the
Franchise
survival guide

Real • World
solutions for
turning your
investment
into a
Money •
Making
Business

Carol B.
Green

PROBUS PUBLISHING COMPANY
Chicago, Illinois
Cambridge, England

ISBN 1-55738-438-X

Printed in the United States of America

BB

2 3 4 5 6 7 8 9 0

This book is dedicated to my husband, Jules, who has always been there to guide, encourage, inspire, and counsel.

Table of Contents

Preface   vii

Acknowledgments   ix

PART ONE: Getting Started in a Franchise Business   1

    CHAPTER 1: The Franchising Evolution   3
    CHAPTER 2: Franchising from the Franchisee
                 Perspective   19
    CHAPTER 3: Sources of Capital to Finance Your Franchise   37

PART TWO: Reach Your Target Market   61

    CHAPTER 4: Analyzing Competition in the 1990s   63
    CHAPTER 5: Changes in Market Conditions   79
    CHAPTER 6: Setting Marketing Goals   93
    CHAPTER 7: Setting Prices   109

PART THREE: Financial Management and Operations   **119**

    CHAPTER 8: Controlling Costs   121
    CHAPTER 9: Managing Your Money Effectively   129
    CHAPTER 10: Purchasing and Inventory Management   149
    CHAPTER 11: Crime as a Business Cost   163
    CHAPTER 12: The Ravages of Nature on Business   185

Conclusion   **203**

Appendix   **205**

Franchising and Business Glossary   **207**

Index   **219**

Preface

In March of 1967 I walked into a Weight Watchers meeting in Newark, Delaware. I had lived in Newark for three years, and had heard of Weight Watchers, mainly from my mom who had lost some weight on the program. I was among the first members to join this new franchise in Delaware. In fact, I had never even heard the word "franchise" before, and didn't have the vaguest idea what it meant, nor what it would mean to me.

When I walked into that Weight Watchers group, I was shy and suffering from very low self-esteem. I was to emerge from the program with three *Es*—I was energized, enthusiastic, and wanted to evangelize the world with my new discovery.

I had been fat since I was seven years old. I started gaining weight after I had my tonsils out. My family just assured me that it was baby fat, and that I'd soon outgrow it. They ignored my compulsive eating and insatiable craving for sweets. I started dieting when I was twelve. By thirteen, I had visited the family doctor and was on diet pills. It was to be some 21 years after I embarked on this "yo-yo" weight loss regimen that I found Weight Watchers.

By now, you possibly think you picked up the wrong book. Is this a diet book in disguise? No, it's really about franchising, and how I gained the knowledge to write this book. Because of that first step into Weight Watchers, I overcame my fears of driving and public speaking, which allowed me to take the next risk—becoming a group leader for Weight Watchers. I was ultimately to lead two groups. One was located in the working-class community of Elsmere; the other catered to faculty and staff at the University of Delaware. The membership was diverse, but they all responded positively to my weekly lectures.

The owners of the Weight Watchers franchise in Delaware took an interest in me. They singled me out, and ultimately offered me a partnership in the Weight Watchers franchise in Virginia. After much investigation and discussion with my family, I opted to fulfill a dream and apply for the Weight Watchers franchise in Denver, Colorado. Going west was a dream I always held on to. My dad had lived in Kansas and Missouri, and I grew up hearing stories of my grandmother's travels to Colorado, Wyoming, Utah, and California.

In early 1968, I applied to Weight Watchers for a franchise. After three weeks of training in New York City, I was granted a franchise for 12 counties in Colorado, known as the "front range" counties. I was soon able to expand that to include Colorado, Wyoming, Western Nebraska, and South Dakota. When I sold the franchise in 1985 to Weight Watchers International (by then a subsidiary of the H.J. Heinz Corporation), I had some 400 employees in the four-state area.

Franchising can allow you to build equity. Thanks to the equity I built in my franchised business, I do not have to work again. I choose to work as a franchise consultant, using the knowledge that I have gained firsthand. My goal in writing this book is to help you who are currently franchisees, or those of you who are aspiring franchisees, to achieve the level of success that you desire, and perhaps exceed your initial aspirations.

My experience tells me that you will receive very focused training from your franchisor. Within a one- to three-week period you will be asked to digest all of the "how-to's" of a specific business. This book is designed to give you the bigger picture—that is, the how-to's of successfully working with your franchisor, learning more about the business world, and how it directly influences the success of your business.

Acknowledgments

I want to gratefully acknowledge the assistance of certain individuals who provided wise counsel. I want to thank my friends Gloria Zigner and Ellie Greenberg for encouraging me to write this book. Gloria took the time to read the manuscript and to share her valuable insights. A special thank you to my personal secretary of many years, Connie Beiser, who stood by to organize the manuscript, and to new friend Terry Savage, who pointed the way to enter the publishing world. Thank you's are also extended to Englewood State Farm Agency owner, John Pifer, who kindly reviewed Chapter 12, and to Jim Henderson, Regional Director of Region 8—Small Business Administration—for his information and review of Chapter 3. Another thank you to the Littleton, Colorado, Police Department for advice on the structuring of the chapter on crime and its impact on business. And a special thank you is in order to Probus editor Marlene Chamberlain for working patiently with me in producing the final manuscript.

PART ONE

Getting Started
in a
Franchise Business

CHAPTER 1

The Franchising Evolution

Franchising is basically a licensing system by which the owner (the Licensor) of a product or service licenses another (the Licensee) to market his product or service within a defined territory following the guidelines established by the licensor.

Starting in the 1970s, legislation was passed that further defined and regulated franchising in the U.S. This legislation mandated that if three components were present in a licensing agreement, it was considered to be a franchise for the purpose of regulation. These components are:

1. The utilizations of a uniform tradename or service mark;

2. A uniform system of operations; and

3. A fee of at least $500 during the first six months of business.

With these components present, the basic franchise relationship is established between the franchisor and franchisee.

Early History of Franchising

Today, franchising is the fastest growing method of doing business in the marketplace, but it is really nothing new. Some believe the institution of franchising dates back at least to the Middle Ages (476 A.D. – 1453 A.D.). At that time, a feudal lord could grant the rights to others to hold markets or fairs, to operate ferries, and to perform some of the activities traditionally carried out by professional and craft guilds. Regulations governing franchises became embedded in the common law of various countries.

During the Middle Ages it was also common practice for governments to offer important people a license or franchise granting them the right to maintain civil law, or to establish and collect tax revenues. The licensee or franchisee paid the franchisor a specified sum from the tax revenues to receive protection from the government. Thus, monarchies controlled lands by giving ongoing protection for a fee.

There are those who say Queen Isabella of Spain invented franchising when she granted Christopher Columbus a "franchise" in 1492 to develop trade with the New World. How ironic that it would eventually be in this "New World" that franchising would be reestablished in the 20th century.

During the 18th and 19th centuries in Europe, similar arrangements were used that were more closely related to business and commerce. Many tavern and pub owners who were experiencing financial hardships turned to the large brewers for financial assistance. In return for their financial aid, a brewer would require that the owners buy all their beer from his brewery. The earliest recorded business franchise was in 1845 in Germany between brewers and tavern owners for exclusive distribution rights of specific brands of ale. This arrangement provided assurance to the tavern owners that they would have a dependable supply of product, and assurance to the brewers that they would have a distribution system in place to deliver their product to the consumer.

Today, the term *franchise* usually refers to the "business format" relationship, in which the franchisor teaches the franchisee the entire business including store layout, merchandising, marketing, selling, inventory structure and control, accounting, and personnel procedures.

Franchising in the United States

In the United States, franchises were particularly prominent in the mid-1800s when street railways and other utilities were evolving, and cities would arrange with specific companies to operate transportation routes and schedule services. Since that time, municipalities and states have granted exclusive franchises to utility and public transportation companies in exchange for the right to regulate the firms' activities. In another more recent example, municipalities and counties have granted franchises to cable companies to exclusively service their market area.

In the U.S., the first true, contractual, commercial franchise using the business format approach is considered to have been the Singer Sewing Machine Company, which formed a franchise in 1851. To solve the "sewing machine war," in which four manufacturers were suing one other, Isaac Singer and his attorney-partner Edward Clark organized the Sewing Machine Combination, America's first patent pool, dividing the distribution rights among them.

As with all successful franchisors, Singer was an energetic promoter with a keen business sense. The firm was an enormous success and had no difficulty selling its product. The business problem it faced was the servicing of its machines. To resolve the dilemma, Singer offered protected territories to individuals, with the exclusive right to sell and service their machines. The structure of the contractual arrangement shows the origins of a modern franchise arrangement. What is particularly significant in this early arrangement was that these franchises were granted worldwide rights. A vital distribution and marketing concept was created, and that concept has evolved into modern, business format franchising as we know it today.

Franchising continued to grow as the industrial revolution in the U.S. began to gain momentum, and as mass production created a need for better distribution systems.

Auto Industry a Franchise Pioneer

Franchising in the auto industry has the longest tenure in our economy. A company that had an early influence on franchising was General Motors. Lacking capital to open retail outlets, it began selling its autos through a system of dealers that is still used in the automobile industry. Among the first General Motors franchisees were the owners of bicycle and hardware stores, who sold cars as a sideline.

When Henry Ford developed mass production of the Model T, he needed an efficient distribution system to get his cars to the customers. Like General Motors, Ford lacked the capital to establish multiple retail outlets in a short period of time, and so the company adopted the franchise system of dealers in as many places as possible. As a result of the success of this type of distribution system, all automobile producers decided to implement this format. Today the automotive industry accounts for a significant percentage of all franchise sales.

Fast Food Gets in the Act

The benefits of the business concept of franchising were widely demonstrated after World War II in the restaurant, hotel, and motel industries. The first big franchising boom came in the 1950s, spurred by the success of some of the famous fast-food franchises.

In 1955, the classic franchise story emerged—McDonald's. A chain of fast-food hamburger restaurants in California was discovered by Ray Kroc, a salesman of a product known as the Multimixer. He sold his machine to ice cream establishments and restaurants. When he started selling the product to McDonald's, he was fascinated by the number of reorders. He decided to observe the operation of the company. What really surprised him was that people stood in long lines to order the foods served by McDonald's.

Kroc went on to license the rights to expand the operation throughout the nation. He combined his insight into the potential for the universal acceptance of this business with high standards of quality control, service, friendliness, and quality. He used his ability to develop new products and advertising to create the giant of the franchise field. However, the most important thing he did was to understand that, by franchising, he could capture the energy of thousands of entrepreneurs to make his dream a reality.

During the same period, Harlan Sanders founded Kentucky Fried Chicken, and in 1959 the International House of Pancakes started selling breakfasts in franchises throughout the country. In this way, the 1950s saw the food service industry quietly embark on a revolution that we take for granted today. These success stories jolted the economic establishment, irreversibly changing America's eating habits and landscapes, as evidenced by the familiar strips of fast food franchises in virtually every town and city.

The 1960s saw much more than just food franchises start up. Numerous types of businesses—hotels, convenience stores, laundries, groceries, business services, and printing operations—began to flourish. In 1970 the franchise industry recorded sales well over $100 billion, which accounted for more than 10 percent of the GNP and over 25 percent of the entire retail sector.[1] By 1975 franchise industry sales had doubled to over $200 billion.[2] 1990 figures were projected to be at almost $716 billion, 114 percent higher than the start of the 1980s.[3]

Franchising Problems

With such a strong influence in the American economy, franchising became a target for shady operators using the franchising concept for illegal gains. While solid companies like McDonald's, KFC, and Hertz were in the process of building legitimate business opportunities, at the same time there were unscrupulous business people taking advantage of the lack of regulation to ensnare unsuspecting individuals into their business opportunities under the guise of franchising. Celebrities were used to promote unproven concepts, and false and unsubstantiated claims were made for various businesses. As is often the case, many honest business people ended up paying for the abuses of a few dishonest ones.

In 1968, when I purchased my Weight Watchers franchise, there was not one franchise regulation in place in the world. I was totally on my own. I knew nothing of the background of the individuals running the franchise, the financial state of the company, or their track record. That changed in the early 1970s when the U.S. Government's small business committees of the House and Senate held hearings concerning fraudulent practices in the franchise industry. Because of these hearings, states began enacting protective legislation regulating the industry. Disclosure and registration requirements were adopted.

State and Federal Regulation

These state regulations started popping up in 1971, beginning in California. Throughout the 1970s, states across the country enacted different regulations to protect would-be buyers of franchises. Now, though, reputable franchisors found themselves plagued by different state regulations, and a number of franchisors worked through the International Franchise Association (IFA) to encourage the Federal government to come up with a set of regulations that would apply to all states.

Although franchising had been around since the 1850s, it wasn't until 1979, with the cooperation of the IFA, that national legislation was passed giving the Federal Trade Commission authority over franchising.

This legislation was Rule 436,[4] designed to replace state regulations. The Rule requires every franchisor that offers franchises in the U.S. to have a disclosure document available to offer to a prospective franchisee. It is also regulates the timing of the presentation of this document to the franchisee. It must be offered at the first meeting between prospective franchisee and franchisor, and it may not be signed by the franchisee prospect until they have had the disclosure document in their possession for at least 10 business days. This delay is designed as a cooling-off period, and to permit the parties to consult with an appropriate party such as a lawyer, accountant, franchise, or business consultant.

In addition, Rule 436 instructs the franchisor on the type of information that must be disclosed to the franchisee. This includes basic information on the nature of the business, its history, its officers and directors and their bankruptcy and litigation history, and businesses they were associated with. Furthermore, audited financials of the franchise, and the costs involved in buying and establishing this business, must be revealed. The rule is in place to protect neophyte franchisees from unscrupulous business people. Reputable franchisors welcomed it. In fact, they worked to enact the legislation to avoid 50 states having 50 different sets of regulations.

The FTC continued to have the monitoring responsibilities associated with the Act, which identifies 20 sections that a disclosure document must have. These required sections, along with mandated financial information, are as follows:

1. Identifying information as to the franchisor

2. The business experience of the franchisor's directors and executive officers

3. Business experience of the franchisor

4. Litigation history of the franchisor

5. Bankruptcy history of the franchisor

6. Description of the franchise

7. Initial funds required to be paid by a franchisee

8. Recurring funds required to be paid by a franchisee (i.e., royalties)

9. Affiliated person the franchisee is required or advised to do business with

10. Obligation to purchase

11. Revenues received by the franchisor in consideration of purchases by a franchisee

12. Financing arrangements

13. Restriction of sale

14. Personal participation required of the franchisee in the operation of the business

15. Termination, cancellation, and renewal of the franchise

16. Statistical information concerning the numbers of franchises and company-owned outlets

17. Representations regarding earning capability

18. Site selection

19. Training program

20. Public figure involvement in the franchise

The document itself states, in part, "Read all of your contract carefully. Buying a franchise is a complicated investment. Take your time to decide. If possible, show your contract and this information to an adviser, like a lawyer or an accountant."

What was especially important about FTC Rule 436 was that it made franchising, to a very large extent, self-policing. This was accomplished by putting in place fines of $10,000 per day per franchisor violation. The threat of such tough financial retaliation had the effect of causing franchisors and would-be franchisors to comply with the legislation. Disgruntled franchisees who believed their rights had been violated had the necessary ammunition and legislation to enable them to sue franchisors, based on supposed violations of the FTC rule.

This system appears to have worked successfully for more than 13 years. Under this FTC rule, franchising has flourished. Further regulatory changes are possible. For instance, there is still a problem in that many of the states that had already enacted legislation regulating franchising left their own regulations in place, but at least the federal regulations headed off any new restrictive state legislation. (See Addendum I for a summary of specific state regulations. If you live in a state that has specific regulations, it is advisable to check with your franchisor to be assured that it has complied with those regulations. You may also take the initiative and check with the state governing authority.)

In the February 17, 1989, issue of *The Wall Street Journal*, a feature article indicated that the FTC is considering a move to preempt state regulations. Should this move materialize, it will considerably ease the expense and burden on franchisors to meet the differing regulations of so many states. How will that impact you as franchisees? It should have a relatively small impact, if we consider the successful track record of the FTC.

Growth of Franchising

Despite becoming more regulated in the 1970s, franchising continued to grow. In 1979, total sales of all franchised business was approximately $115 billion from approximately 400,000 franchise outlets. The franchising boom had slowed from the middle to the close of the decade. Unfortunately, by that time, many small business people had invested their resources in franchise concepts that were misleading, misrepresentative, or fraudulent, and thousands of operators went out of business.

In the 1980s, with new laws governing franchising, the industry established new credibility. FTC laws made it more difficult to franchise with the sole purpose of fraudulent intent. Franchising began to prosper in what was seen as a second boom. In fact, most experts believe that growth accelerated in the 1980s because of regulation. It discouraged get-rich-quick types and encouraged franchisors committed to long-term growth.

Success Rates

Another important reason for renewed interest and growth in franchising is the success rate of franchisees compared with other small businesses. An unfortunate but true statistic is that more than 65 percent of small businesses never survive to their fifth year. According to A. Vernon Weaver, former administrator of the U.S. Small Business Administration, 1,000 small firms go out of business every day. In fact, of all new firms, more than 23 percent will fail in their first two years in business. This information is the result of a study of a sample of the 458 million firms entered into the data base of the Small Business Administration.[5] This high rate of failure is often due to lack of good management skills and/or lack of proper capital.

One basic fact is indisputable. The statistics for franchisees are significantly better. Franchises have recorded less than a 5 percent annual failure rate. This is substantiated by two recent studies. A 1991 study by Arthur Andersen & Co. of 366 franchise companies, small and large, in 60 industries, revealed that nearly 86 percent of all franchise operations opened in the last five years are still under the same ownership. Only 3 percent of these businesses are no longer in operation. Jeffrey E. Kolton, of FranData Corporation, a company that specializes in franchise research, analysis, and document retrieval, presented a new study of franchise termination rates to the U.S. House of Representatives Small Business Committee of June 17, 1992. It revealed that an average of only 4.2 percent of franchisees leave a franchise system on an annual basis.[6]

This low failure rate is attributed to the actual format of assistance franchisees receive from their franchisors. Many of the problems franchisees experience already have been dealt with and solved by the franchisor at some point beforehand. The franchisor can be an inexpensive business consultant, guide, and good friend. As a result, franchising has become the safest way for many small businesses to expand and survive.

The New Franchisees

The 1980s changing life-styles also helped spur the second franchise boom. As a result of increased computerization, global competition, and long periods of recession, many large corporations began to downsize and lay off management staff, and a surge in entrepreneurship began. Many bright, skilled, managerial people wanted to own their own business. Franchising offered a business system for these people with less risk than starting a business of their own.

The 1990s continue to look bright in terms of franchise opportunities. The same underlying causes of growth that impacted the 1980s continue to attract interest in franchise opportunities today. 1993 started with announcements from General Motors, Sears, and IBM of major layoffs numbering in the tens of thousands of employees.

These are the same skilled employees who fueled franchising in the 1980s. Large companies continue downsizing. People no longer believe they have long-term security with large companies. Smaller companies with greater flexibility and commitment to niche markets continue to grow, prosper, and provide employment opportunities.

Middle-management people became ideal candidates for franchises. They were well-educated, ambitious, hard working, and had already bought into the American Dream of increased prosperity. They felt abandoned by large companies, but did not have the entrepreneurial skills to start businesses from scratch. As team players, they made ideal franchisees, and joined the ranks of independent business people in record numbers in the 1980s and 1990s.

One example of these new franchisees is Lee Catalfamo, who was a nuclear engineer working as plant engineer for Public Service Electric & Gas in New Jersey. Although he was well educated and received promotions within the corporation, he never was able to meet his expectations in terms of authority. Early in 1988, he made the decision to strike out on his own in order to have more control in his business life. After careful consideration, he determined that a franchise offered less risk. It seemed to him that it was safer than starting a business from scratch.

He chose AMBIC, a building inspection franchise, because this type of business matched his skills and his strong technical background. He knew he did not want a lot of employees and administrative responsibilities. He already had experienced that in corporate life. An AMBIC franchise didn't require responsibilities in these areas. Catalfamo has gone on to develop a successful AMBIC franchise in his area, and a satisfying career as well.

George Kunzman found himself being offered a financial benefits package to retire when IBM opted to reduce the size of the corporate staff. He decided that the solution provided an opportunity and determined he would use the money to enter into his own business. He narrowed the choices down to printing and package shipping businesses. He considered starting a business on his own. However, like Catalfamo and countless others, he opted for franchising in order to reduce the risk. He ultimately selected The Packaging Store (sometimes referred to as Handle With Care Packaging Store) and opened his store in Boca Raton, Florida. Kunzman believes the excellent training and support he received from the Packaging Store franchisor has made the difference in his success. He has opted not to buy additional franchises, but to focus on the growth of his one store. He remains enthusiastic and optimistic about the future of his single-unit franchise business.

The continuance of middle and senior managerial layoffs, forced early retirements, and severance packages for some of those being outplaced has been compounded in the 1990s with the longest peacetime recession in history. Late 1991, 1992, and early 1993 have brought record personnel cutbacks from large corporations, releasing even more middle managers into the marketplace. Since entire industries have been impacted as well, many of these people have lost access to quick job replacement. If you are a displaced corporate executive and are the sole supporter of your family, you fit the description of the latest wave of prospects seeking to enter franchising. According to an article in the November 1991 issue of Nation's Business, during the last several years U.S. corporations have laid off over 500,000 white-collar workers. According to a 1991 survey by S&S Franchise Marketing Consultants, based in Chicago, 70 percent of current inquiries regarding franchises come from this group of laid-off white-collar workers.

Is Franchising for You?

Perhaps you recognize yourself in this group. You may already be a franchisee who joined the ranks of small business after leaving a larger corporation. Perhaps you even made this choice after being outplaced. I have personally worked with outplaced managers from IBM, Martin Marietta, U.S. West, National Demographics, Manville, and countless other firms. These men and women have decided that franchising provided the perfect entree to starting up a business.

You will find certain benefits from a franchise arrangement if you have a solid franchisor to back you. Your franchisor should provide you with business systems, the research and development of new products, store design and layout, access to cost-effective equipment and products, marketing and promotional materials, and access to larger markets.

On the other hand, there are many things a franchisor cannot do for you, as your contractual agreement requires that you maintain an independent business relationship. You must run your business, access capital, penetrate markets, cut costs, and manage your money. This book is designed to help you do this.

The Boom Continues

If you're wondering if this is a good time to get into franchising, if the boom is continuing, know that franchise sales of goods and services in more than 542,000 outlets were forecast at $757.8 billion in 1991 according to "Franchising In The Economy 1991," a study prepared by Horwath International for the International Franchise Association Educational Foundation. This was 114 percent over the level of sales at the start of the 1980s.[7] The latest available figures show that in 1991, growth of franchisee-owned units was projected to grow at the rate of 6.2 percent over 1990 figures. It also was projected that franchising will encompass 35 percent of all retail sales in 1991. That is the first time this figure will be achieved.[8] Employment in franchising, including part-time workers and working proprietors, was projected at more than 7.3 million at the end of 1988. It is projected that income from franchises makes up almost 20 percent of the gross national product of the U.S.[9]

Note the following charts. They have been included to give you a visual perspective of the growth of franchising and its impact on the economy. Reviewing the numbers from year to year clearly demonstrates the rate of growth, in addition to the dollar impact on our economy. Figure 1-1 features the growth of total sales for all franchising, 1980 to 1991.[10] Figure 1-2 demonstrates the growth of total

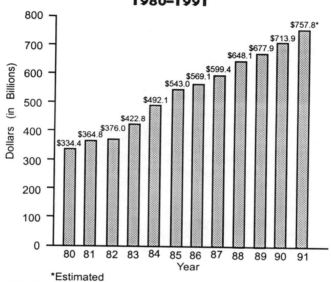

Figure 1-1
Total Sales—All Franchising USA
1980–1991

*Estimated

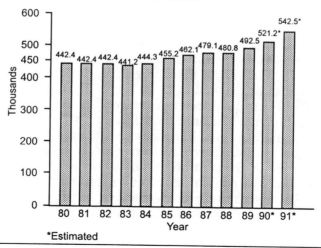

Figure 1-2
Total Establishments—All Franchising USA
1980–1991

*Estimated

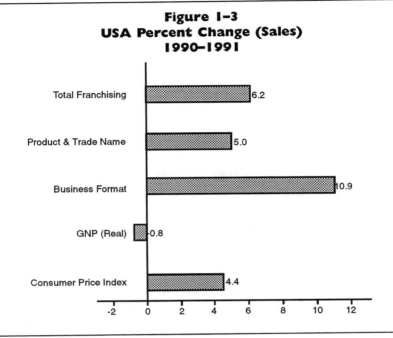

Figure 1-3
USA Percent Change (Sales)
1990-1991

establishments for all franchises, 1980 to 1991.[11] Finally, Figure 1-3 features the percentage change in all sales from 1990 to 1991.[12]

The 1990s have made franchising the single greatest export of the United States. This is a business system that, when it's done correctly, works beneficially for the franchisor and the franchisee. It permits the franchisor to expand regionally, nationally, and even internationally with relatively little capital. It also permits individuals to be part of a proven business system with major business presence in the marketplace.

While Americans have become entrepreneurs since Plymouth Rock and Jamestown, some of the rules and the dreams have changed as society has also changed. We can no longer operate as if we had a captive audience that must buy our fish or starve through the winter. There is competition extraordinaire among small businesses! There are government rules and regulations (from OSHA to tax credits). There's subliminal advertising and more sophisticated marketing techniques. More and more small businesses need to be concerned about public relations. There's mail-order competition. In short, there are 1,001 factors—internal and external—that can affect the small business owner's success and sometimes help ensure his failure.

Even those who choose the franchise route are not completely protected and shepherded. A franchisee realistically cannot expect her franchisor to be there at every step of the growth process. The franchisor cannot be expected to be knowledgeable about every aspect of the business world, let alone the franchisee and her local economy.

Making Franchising Spell Success

This book takes a macro view of business matters that should directly benefit you in the running of your business. This book is designed to help result in better financial remuneration and longer-term success. Years ago, business wasn't as complicated as it is today. If you wanted to open a shoe repair shop, or a dressmaker's shop, or whatever, you just got your plan together and hung out a shingle. You would have been able to succeed in a relatively small community without having an in-depth understanding of business conditions on a city, county, state, or national level—or even international level.

Things have changed. Today it is as risky to jump into the business arena without experience as it would be to ski outside the out-of-bounds markers. As small businesspersons, like our counterparts in moderate and large businesses, we are going to have to develop some understanding of economic and market conditions. It's a necessity if we want our businesses to survive and flourish in the 1990s.

Franchise businesses do differ. A Dunhill Office Personnel franchise differs from a Grease Monkey, as does a Signs By Tomorrow from a Wendy's. However, the commonalities are strong, and this book will address them. As franchisees, we're team players. Our franchisor is our coach. This book will lay out the game plans and the rules to help you be a winner.

ENDNOTES

[1] Church, Nancy Subway, *Future Opportunities in Franchising: A Realistic Appraisal* (N.V.: Pilot Ind., Inc.) 1979 pp. 12.

[2] "Franchising In The Economy: 1983–1985." Published by the U.S. Dept. of Commerce. Washington, D.C.

[3] "Franchising In The Economy." Published by the International Franchise Association Educational Foundation, Inc., Washington D.C.

[4] Federal Trade Commission Franchise Rule Summary, Bureau of Consumer Protection, Washington, D.C., 1979.

[5] "The State of Small Business: A Report To The President," delivered to Congress, 1989. United States Government Printing Office, 1989.

[6] *The Info Franchise Newsletter*, Vol. 16, No. 8, August 1992, Info Press, Inc., Lewiston NY, pp. 2–3.

[7] "Franchising In the Economy 1991," published by the International Franchise Association Foundation, Inc., and Horwath International, Washington, D.C., 1991.

[8] Ibid.

[9] "Franchising In the Economy 1988–1990," published by the International Franchise Association Foundation, Inc., and Horwath International, Washington, D.C., 1990.

[10] "Franchising In the Economy 1991."

[11] Ibid.

[12] Ibid.

CHAPTER 2

Franchising from the Franchisee Perspective

The individual or business granting the business rights is called the franchisor. The individual or business receiving the opportunity to operate in accordance with the chosen method to produce and/or sell the product or service is the franchisee. Franchising enables the franchisor to expand a successful business and plan of operation from a single unit to a large operation with multiple locations. For the franchisee, the benefits are acquiring a proven business system, training, pooled advertising power, brand name or service recognition, good will, and the continuing assistance from corporate experts in the specific franchised business.

Franchising is a unique, relatively safe, and proven way for people with limited capital to start up and operate their own business. Franchising also permits small, independent businesses to associate with a larger organization that has name recognition in the market and a proven track record. Franchises can utilize the training, techniques, trade secrets, and proven operational procedures of a larger, successful, established business. Franchising also permits a group to market their goods and services in a cost-efficient manner, developing added clout and visibility through association. This association often also permits beneficial group purchasing discounts locally and nationally.

Selecting a Franchise

Before considering the purchase of a franchise, you should recognize that franchising is not for everyone. If you are a true entrepreneur, you will be better off starting or buying an established business of your own. Why? Because franchising, at its best, has been designed for corporate management people. These are people who have been comfortable in a corporate, team-oriented setting. When you buy a franchise, you join a team. The true entrepreneur usually wants to call the shots, to be the innovator. In franchising, that is the area of responsibility of the franchisor. Some are open-minded and responsive to franchisee input; some are not. If you are in the latter setting, you will feel constrained and, more than likely, be unhappy.

If you do opt to buy a franchise, fortunately, there are tools you can use, including a number of franchise opportunities handbooks available in libraries and in most bookstores. They alphabetically list most franchises for sale in the U.S., then break them out by categories such as automotive, construction, food, home entertainment products, insurance, maid services, weight control, etc. They do not, however, break the franchises out into all conceivable categories. For instance, you may want to think about home-based businesses or mobile-based businesses, but these are mixed throughout the categories of franchises in these books.

Each listing summarizes the franchise. The summary includes such information as company name, address, phone number, key personnel dealing in franchise sales, description of the business they are in, length of time franchising, number of company-owned and franchised units in existence, franchise fee, franchise royalty, and total investment. Unfortunately, since these books are published annually, and the information is gathered throughout the year, the information is often quite old. Nevertheless, it is a starting point.

Other starting points are the weekly franchise ads that appear Thursday in *The Wall Street Journal* classifieds, or Wednesday in *USA*

Today. This is not to say that ads do not appear every day, but that on these particular days these papers carry an especially high concentration of advertisements for franchises.

Using a Franchise Broker

Another source of help is from franchise brokers. Most represent one to four franchises, and specifically promote these. You may find yourself dealing with such a specialized broker when you respond to a newspaper advertisement. Single-unit broker-representatives are usually employees of the franchisor. Multiple representatives are usually independent contractor-brokers.

There are fewer than 100 companies, such as the one that I am affiliated with, that represent a large numbers of franchises through an affiliation with the Franchise Broker's Network. The Network represents 100+ diverse franchisors and licensors. Companies affiliated with the Franchise Broker's Network focus on the individual who is buying the franchise rather than starting from the point of representing a specific franchise. They look at you, your interests, education, abilities, preferred work hours (i.e., no weekends, please), and the amount of money you have to invest. I like to compare their role to that of a real estate broker. Although paid by the seller, the real estate broker also has to satisfy the buyer.

A buyer comes in looking to buy a three-bedroom house on a quarter-acre in Aurora, Colorado, and can afford to buy a house for $125,000. The job of the real estate broker is to find the buyer's dream home. The same is true of the potential franchise buyer. Say you are strong in business-to-business sales. You want such a service business in Aurora, Colorado, that is office-based and in which you could invest from $75,000 to $125,000. The specialized broker researches companies that fit your specific guidelines.

Examine Your Motivation

Another important step is determining your motivation. Are you buying a franchise to increase your income? Do you want to travel less than is currently required on your job, perhaps to spend more time with your family? Are you looking for more relaxation? Perhaps more hands-on work? Some people want more management responsibilities, others want less. Everyone, it appears, wants more control over their lives. Think long and hard about what it is that you're looking for. That knowledge will help provide needed criteria for a successful decision.

Contact Prospective Franchisors

If you are researching on your own, the next step is contacting the companies that interest you. You may call or write. Should you write, you most likely will receive a phone call from the franchisor pre-qualifying you as a likely candidate for the business. Should you pass muster, you will receive an informational and often colorful brochure highlighting the advantages of selecting this particular business opportunity. You then will be encouraged to fill out a detailed and confidential questionnaire. Some of the questions will inquire about your work background, education, interests, and references. You will be asked to fill out a financial statement and to provide financial references.

The franchisor then will send you a disclosure document, or will ask that you make an appointment to visit their headquarters in order to receive this disclosure document. If you are serious, you should plan to visit the headquarters. You will want to know more about management, their procedures, ethics, and business philosophy.

They, of course, will want to know more about you. Be honest! In the pre-screening, they only will screen out people who do not fit their profile. A good company doesn't want you to fail. If they believe that you are the wrong person for their franchise, it is to both your advantages not to associate with each other. Don't take a rejection personally. The experienced franchisor has a good idea who will and who will not succeed in their franchise. They are doing you a favor in this elimination process. Everyone wants a good marriage. No one wants a painful and costly divorce.

Questions to Ask About Franchising

I am recommending that you ask the franchisors specific questions about their operation. There are also general questions to be asked about franchising. The International Franchise Association (IFA) has prepared a brochure with the 21 most commonly asked questions about franchising. Contact the IFA at 1350 New York Avenue, Suite 900, Washington D.C. 20005 for this brochure. Examples:

1. How does a franchise chain start?

2. How widespread is franchising?

3. Is there now a glut of franchises in the marketplace, or is franchising still growing?

4. What kind of investment is necessary to buy a franchise?

5. What is the Federal Trade Commission Rule?

We have attempted in this book to address these questions.

Evaluating Franchise Opportunities

Be sure it's a business that is appealing. Unlike a job, you cannot walk away by simply quitting. You will have made a financial and contractual commitment to operate this business.

Check out the company. Evaluate the franchisor, its reputation, and business record. Examine its system of franchising and its status in the industry, and your own competence and motivations in relation to that industry.

What are your qualifications? Are you physically qualified? Do you have the right experience, education, learning capacity, temperament, and financial status?

Are you going to actively participate in this business, or are you planning to be an investor? Do you have partners or other key people lined up to assist you, if necessary? If not, will the franchisor help you with staffing guidelines, training guidelines, etc.?

Have you talked to current franchisees of the company? The law requires that when the franchisor gives a prospective franchisee their disclosure document, they must include a list of all current franchisees by name, and the list must be updated quarterly. That means you can call these franchisees, and you absolutely should. Ask them if they would buy this franchise again, if they knew then what they know today. Ask them if the training was satisfactory, outstanding? Ask how good the support services of the franchisor are. Are they making the kind of money they anticipated? Some will be specific in their responses, other will not. Nevertheless, ask. Don't be shy. You are going to be investing a major part of your net worth into this business. You need answers.

Corporate Management

It is most important to have confidence in the management of this company. Markets change, as do economic conditions, as does competition. You need to feel confident that management can make the necessary business adjustments to assure your success now and in the future. Who are these people? Have they failed in businesses and filed bankruptcy? This information is available in the franchise disclosure document. Meet the managers. Ask questions. Don't be humble. This is your future we're talking about.

Other important data you need to check are the audited financials of the company, which should be included in the disclosure document. Look at financial stability, growth, and the source of income. You don't want to buy into a franchise that is being supported through franchise fees instead of product sales and royalties. The reason is that a franchise that is forced to sell franchises in order to survive is going to sell franchises to anyone. That translates into a situation where their motivations and their franchise team is compromised.

An important exception to this rule is among young franchisors. Their royalties are at the lowest level they will ever be. They have the fewest franchises at the lowest level of the sales curve. Naturally their royalties are very low. Don't eliminate them on this basis. You must consider the risk/reward aspect of early entry. I bought Weight Watchers when it was a young franchise. There was higher risk at this stage. However, had I waited, I would have been out of the picture. Fewer than 100 franchises were sold nationwide, and prime areas were sold out quickly. If I had not bought into the young franchisor, I would have missed out on what became a million dollar opportunity.

Approach your selection with care and concern, but not fear. The information is available for you today. Take advantage of it.

Business Format Franchising

According to the Federal Trade Commission, franchising is seen as a continuing commercial relationship that can be either one of two types. With the first type—the business format franchise—the franchise opportunity consists of three major components:

1. The first component exists when the franchisee operates under the franchisor's trademark, service mark, trade name, and advertising or any other commercial symbol designating the franchisor ("mark").

2. The second component is the ability of the franchisor to exercise significant control over, or to give to the franchisee significant assistance in, the franchisor's methods of operation.

3. The third component is that the franchisee is required to make a payment of $500 or more to the franchisor or a person affiliated with the franchisor, at any time before or within six months after the business opens. When these three elements are present, regardless of whether the business is called a franchise, a license, a dealership, or whatever, the Federal Trade Commission considers it to be a franchise in terms of governance.

Business format franchising is concerned with the business opportunity, the method that includes trademark, product, service marketing plans, managerial controls, quality control, and training programs. This type of franchising really focuses on the format to be used by the franchisee and has been responsible for the growth associated with franchising since the 1950s. The number of business format franchisors was approximately 900 in 1972.[1] The average annual growth rate of business format franchises was 15 percent during the 1972-1978 period and should remain at the 1979-1985 rate of 11.5 percent for the next five years. Currently there are more than 3,000 operating business format franchisors.[2]

This growth really can be seen in the rapid expansion in the restaurant, food service, motel/hotel, printing, retailing, and real estate sectors. The reasons for such a boom in these areas parallel the shift in the U.S. economy—away from the manufacturing and production of goods to the provision of services. The service environment has been created, and it lends itself especially well to franchising. It has encouraged the development of franchises, especially those that focus on providing services oriented to current lifestyles.

Most of the new franchise agreements are of the business format type. The number of business format franchise units in operation as of 1990 was approximately 521,215. Based on the projected growth rate from 1989 to 1990 of 5.4 percent,[3] we can project that there will be more than 600,000 units by the end of 1993.

Product and Trade Name Franchises

The second type of franchise is known as the trade name or product franchise. In this case, the franchisee sells goods or services that are supplied by the franchisor or a person affiliated with the franchisor. The franchisor assists the franchisee in securing locations or sites for vending machines or rack displays, or providing the service of a person able to do either. Also, the franchisee is required to make a payment of $500 or more to the franchisor, or a person affiliated with the franchisor, at any time before to within six months after the business initiates operations.[4]

Trade name and product franchising accounted for about 71 percent of all franchised sales in 1987, or approximately $421 billion in sales.[5] This type of franchising appears to be in decline. From 1989 to 1990 this group actually declined 3 percent, or from 139,245 units to 135,097 units.[6] These franchise categories (automobile dealers, gasoline service stations, and soft drink bottlers) are characterized by saturation of the market, intense advertising competition, availability, and price. A specific example of this decline is the move by the large oil companies not to renew the independent trade name gasoline franchises, replacing them with company-owned operations.

Multiple Franchise Structure

It helps to understand the structure of franchising if you plan to buy a franchise or expand your current operation. The following two diagrams illustrate the point.

We start with the franchisor, the party that sells the trademark and business format system while providing ongoing support and services. The master franchisee holds the rights to a geographical market. I owned a master franchise for Weight Watchers of the Rocky Mountain Region. It included the states of Colorado, Wyoming, Western Nebraska, and South Dakota. A sub-franchisor has the same rights as a master franchisee, but is also responsible for

Figure 2-1
Sub-Franchising Model

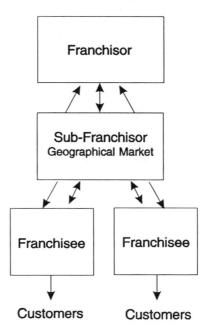

- Sets trademark and business format with a "territory" to sub-franchisor in exchange for franchise fee and royalty. Little or no direct contact with franchisees.
- Responsible for setting and servicing franchisees with a given territory. Receives franchise fee and royalties, and shares with franchisor.
- Owns and operates individual franchise. Pays franchise fee in exchange for business format, trademark, and support from the sub-franchisor.*

---

*   "Multi-Level Franchising: How Far? How Fast?" *Franchising World Magazine*, Jan./Feb. 1988.

selling sub-franchises, training, and servicing the franchisees in his area. This is the most popular format for international franchising today. The sub-franchisor takes the rights to a country, and sells franchises within the country. The area developer has similar rights to a sub-franchisor. In the case of an area developer, she signs a contract for a specific geographical area and agrees to open and operate a specific number of franchises within that area. She often

Figure 2-2
Master Franchising and Area Developer Model

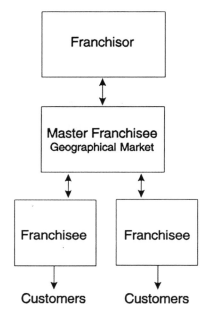

- Sells trademark and business format system and geographical market to master franchisee. Provides services and continuing support to franchisees through master or area developer. Shares franchise fee and royalty with master franchisee or area developer.
- Controls geographical market and develops master through selling additional franchises and servicing current franchisees. Receives share of franchise fee and royalties and, in some cases, advertising fees.
- Owns and operates individual franchise. Pays franchise fee and royalties directly to franchisor for business format, trademark, and continuing support from franchisor.*

---

* "Multi-Level Franchising: How Far? How Fast?" *Franchising World Magazine*, Jan./Feb. 1988.

---

can open these franchises herself, or sell off the rights to individual franchisees. There usually is a schedule involved in the development agreement. The agreement could say that she must open 10 stores in three years: four in Year One; three in Years Two and Three. Should the area developer fail to meet that schedule, the franchisor usually reassumes these rights in accordance with their contract. However, the area developer is not penalized as to successful, previous development, and will have full rights to all contractual obligations met prior to the default. The last player is the one that we are most familiar with, the unit franchisee. This party owns and operates an individual franchise.[7]

Franchise Relationships

The close working relationship between the franchisor and the franchisee is the most critical aspect of franchising. Success for both depends on the synergy of this relationship. Both parties should understand the interdependence in the relationship. Respecting that interdependence, and building on the strengths within the organization, goes a long way toward assuring the success of the entire franchise operation.

At the outset of this franchisee-franchisor relationship, franchisors are somewhat like nurturing parents and franchisees like dependent children. Once the franchisee masters the basics of what the franchisor is teaching, the relationship becomes more balanced. In most cases, franchisees are obligated contractually to pay the franchisor an initial fee and a royalty for the length of the franchise agreement. Franchisors should continually offer an array of valuable services to meet the franchisee's changing needs. If this relationship is not clearly understood or is mismanaged by the franchisor, the seeds of distrust and disharmony can begin to adversely affect communication, as well as the all-important relationship.

The U.S. House Committee on Small Business issued a report on August 13, 1990, indicating that the federal government's focus on disclosure has diverted attention from the issues related to the franchisor-franchisee relationship.[8] The report noted "Franchising has been called the most dynamic business arrangement since the emergence of the corporation a century ago. It is heralded as a dominating force in the distribution of goods and services and the 'wave of the future' for the marketplace . . .."[9] Today, the International Franchise Association is focused on the improvement of the franchisor-franchisee relationship. Communication regarding the different perspectives of specific situations influencing the relationship has been the focus. This is no easy matter, since franchises from different industries have differing areas of contention and concern.

Most recently, there have been allegations by some franchisees regarding the termination and renewal clauses in their contract. This has led to a move for increased franchise regulation. In Iowa, legislation has been introduced that would actually reinterpret existing franchise contracts. As this movement is at an early stage, it would be inappropriate to evaluate the outcome. Franchisors and franchisees alike have taken this renewed movement toward increased regulation seriously. The fear is that a major change in relationships, or a change that precipitates confrontation, will be harmful to all associated with franchising.

Benefits of Franchising

Franchisors initially contract and promise to teach their system of operations to franchisees. They train the franchisee to do what they have done successfully. Equally important, they demonstrate how to avoid situations that have been disasters in their business development.

Florida-based Packaging Store franchisee, George Kunzman, left IBM to invest in a franchised business. He contemplated starting a business from scratch, but ultimately decided that he couldn't afford to make mistakes in starting a new business. He had a family to consider, and he didn't want to fail. He believed it was worth paying the franchisor and to learn from their successes as well as to avoid their mistakes. He opened his Packaging Store in Boca Raton and continues to focus his energies on the growth and success of his business.

A key area of support most retail-based franchisors offer is site selection. Finding the best available site to locate a business is a key to the eventual success of the franchise. Many an entrepreneur has sealed the fate of their business before they have ever opened the door for business through poor site selection and/or lease negotiation. Add to this the training offered by the franchisor, equipment packages made available to the franchisee at beneficial prices, the initial marketing plan, and specific initial advertising—all provide a way for the franchisee to get in gear efficiently and quickly, develop a client base, and move toward profitability.

Franchising provides the means for a person to own and to operate a business using a format that is simple enough to be transferred to another party. When properly executed, franchising helps both parties realize earnings and profit potential. However, it is important to evaluate the situation and important factors associated with the business opportunity before committing yourself to a franchise relationship. In this specific relationship, there are certain advantages and certain risks involved.

Franchise Advantages

Most franchisees agree that franchising is successful for several major reasons.

1. The amount of "added value" and personal assistance from the franchisor given to the franchisee. You are receiving the experience of the franchisor in a nutshell called training. Add this to the amount of hard work and commitment put into the new business on your end and you have the formula for franchise success.

2. The enormous amount of preparation put into opening a single unit. The training period is included in the pre-opening preparation. During that period the franchisee learns how to initiate, operate, and control the functions of the business he is planning to open.

3. The continuing advice in the form of technical and managerial assistance provided by the franchisor (includes ongoing training).

4. The quality control procedures imposed on franchisees by the franchisor. Such controls assure uniform product or services throughout the whole system. Today, "quality assurance" is a catch phrase designed to put American companies back on the quality path. The question of quality and standards has always been a concern of reputable franchisors. The father of contemporary franchising, Ray Kroc of McDonald's, considered quality a prime ingredient to the success of his company.

5. The amount of cash it generally takes to begin a franchised business as opposed to an independent business.

6. The benefit franchisees often get from the franchisor's group power to buy supplies at lower costs, thus obtaining a higher profit margin.

7. The continued research and development by the franchisor of products/services in order to keep franchisees competitive.

8. A potential advantage—a guarantee from the franchisor that no competition from any other franchisee or company-owned outlet will take place in the specific territory agreed upon.

9. Brand name recognition. Think about driving into a strange town, knowing no one and selecting a stop for lunch. Chances are you'll select a familiar franchisor location, rather than stop at an unknown spot.

10. Improved access to capital.

These advantages generally are found throughout the franchise industry, but are not necessarily advantages for *all* franchise operations. The common link with all these aspects comes down to *assistance* from the franchisor.

Franchise Risks

Generally most franchise agreements work out well for both the franchisor and franchisee. The franchising approach intends to help promote profits and develop a healthy and prosperous business, but like most things in life, there are potential risks associated with franchising. Here are some that you should be aware of:

1. There is always an element of risk in starting any business venture.

2. Some franchisors may actually promise certain assistance and then not follow through. Thus the franchisee's needs are not met. No matter how good the opportunity, always play devil's advocate and ask tough questions. That does not mean you should be adversarial. The franchisor could misinterpret your motives and decide that you are an "undesirable" addition to his franchise system.

3. Avoid hype. Some franchisors may have a fantastic business concept that is flourishing. Because of the hype to get into some very successful enterprises, some potential franchisees do not carefully investigate what they are getting into and do

not know what they are legally bound to. It is the obligation of the potential franchisee to use the cooling-off period to read the disclosure document and to consult with appropriate professionals for advice. The correctly prepared disclosure document must include the list of current franchises, with their addresses and phone numbers updated quarterly. Take advantage and call these franchisees. The key question to ask: "Would you buy this franchise again, if you knew then what you know now?"

4. Realistic expectations. If the franchisor does not give the degree of assistance to the franchisee that was anticipated by the franchisee, then the franchisee could consider the royalties one pays to the franchisor to be unjust. At times, this attitude leads to breakaway franchisees and costly litigation. This can often be avoided with good franchisee-franchisor communications.

5. Over-dependence on the franchisor. Another potential disadvantage associated with franchising is that some new franchisees can become overly dependent on the franchisor. This can lead to some franchisees becoming unable to make appropriate common sense decisions. When the franchisor tries to correct the problem, relations can be damaged. It should be made clear that franchising offers broad uniform guidelines that should be followed, yet each local market has variations that should be dealt with at the local level without the advice of the franchisor.

6. In some communities where there are multiple franchise units with different franchisee-owners, the performance of one unit could affect all the units. If a franchisee proves to be a poor operator, it could have adverse impact on customers in the whole community.

International Franchising

It is already a major U.S. export. There are hundreds of U.S. franchisors doing business overseas with tens of thousands of outlets. The USSR even opened its doors to franchisors in 1989. You can find McDonald's in Japan, Weight Watchers in Spain, Burger King in

Germany, Postal Instant Press (PIP) in the United Kingdom, Pizza Hut in Argentina, and on and on.

In the 1990s, countries as diverse as Mexico and China have complied with international trademark law in order to attract franchisors. The expansion into foreign markets by franchisors continues to increase rapidly. In 1988, almost 17 percent of all U.S. business format franchisors had more than 35,000 outlets outside the United States. In addition, domestic product and trade name franchisors are now operating in over 160 countries. This further supports my premise that franchising is a major export of the U.S.,and will continue to be into the 21st century.

Franchise Advisory Councils

One very positive aspect relating to the improvement of franchisor-franchisee relationships has been the creation of franchise advisory councils. As franchise businesses grew, differences of opinion developed as franchisees and franchisors looked at issues from their own perspectives. Franchise advisory councils arose within many franchises. For example, SuperCuts and Weight Watchers formed a franchise advisory council from among their membership. These were open to all of their franchisees. In some cases, regional groups organized to better handle advertising and promotions on a local level. Sometimes these councils developed as a result of dissatisfaction among franchisees, and thereby provided negotiating forums. In a more positive light, many enlightened franchisors understood that differences existed, and moved to initiate advisory councils to provide a vehicle for input to decision making and a forum for dialogue. Tricia Sheriff, president and franchisee of Foliage Design Systems of Birmingham, Alabama, is also president of the Foliage Design Systems Franchisee Advisory Council. She says the council is a positive experience for everyone and has helped the franchisees and the franchisor develop good communication. Foliage Design Systems, a franchise based in Ocala, Florida, is the second largest interiorscape firm in the country. Interiorscaping is the business of providing artistic and appropriate plants and flowers to interior spaces, along with ongoing maintenance contracts. The company sees its strength in their numbers. Their name is becoming identified with outstanding product and maintenance, especially as they acquire an increasing number of national contracts. The franchisees of Foliage Design

Systems view the advisory council as a means to contribute to the research and development of the company's new products and services, its strategic planning, and the conceptualization of new sales and marketing techniques.

Franchises frequently form committees designed to elicit input on specific aspects of the business. When with Weight Watchers International, I chaired a committee of 12 franchisees that developed the first "new" eating program that was introduced for members of the Weight Watchers classes. The original eating plan had been developed by a physician in 1937 and was dated in terms of products and life-styles. The franchisee committee designed an ideal weight-control program. The nutritional staff of Weight Watchers International tested and modified it for introduction to the membership. This was accomplished by the franchise advisory council working closely with the franchisor. The council provided this positive opportunity for both franchisor and franchisee, and most importantly, for the business in general.

Another example of this team effort is how the Foliage Design Franchise Advisory Council targeted the short-term event industry, such as banquets and weddings, as a growth area for their businesses. Together with the franchisor, a plan is being developed to expand this industry. Sociologists tell us that one out of every two marriages fails. This rather disturbing figure deals with relationships on an individual basis. However, franchising requires the managing of relationships or "marriages" with many individuals who have different needs and values at the same time. The objective is to manage these franchise relationships in such a way as to assure the success of the relationship. As with one-on-one relationships, that means good communication, identification of common goals, and the predominance of win/win decision making.

Prospective franchisees must understand clearly the commitment they must make to support and maintain effective, healthy, and harmonious relationships, and to avoid "divorces," which can include both expensive litigation and extensive damage to the franchise system. The relationship, both from the franchisor and franchisee perspectives, must be a responsive, continuing dialogue in order for the franchising system to work.

ENDNOTES

[1] *The Future of Franchising, A Study for the International Franchise Association*, The Naisbitt Group, Washington, D.C., December 1985.

[2] *The 1992 Franchise Annual*, The Info Press, Inc., Canada, 1991.

[3] Federal Trade Commission, *Franchise Rule Summary*, Bureau of Consumer Protection, Washington, D.C., 1979.

[4] *Franchising In the Economy 1988–1990*, International Franchise Association Foundation, Inc. and Horwath International, Washington, D.C., 1990.

[5] Ibid.

[6] *The 1992 Franchise Annual*, The Info Press, Inc., Canada, 1991.

[7] Ibid.

[8] *Franchising In the U.S. Economy: Prospects and Problems.* U.S. House of Representatives Committee on Small Business, August 13, 1990.

[9] Ibid.

CHAPTER 3

Sources of Capital to Finance Your Franchise

When you're in the market to buy a franchise, to open additional units, or to expand your operation, you are going to need capital.

We all know that the most common way for a small business to get capital is to obtain a traditional loan at a traditional commercial bank. However, when loan money appears impossible to access, there are many alternative sources of capital you should be familiar with. For example, when the Federal Reserve Board exerts pressure on banks to restrict credit, the interests of small businesses won't receive any special protection. The simple fact is that, when banks have a choice (and they certainly do during restrictive loaning periods), it is more likely that they will be inclined to lend their "tight money" to larger, more established, and lower-risk businesses rather than small businesses or franchises.

As a business owner, you must broaden considerably your understanding of alternative as well as traditional sources of capital, including the pros and cons of each choice. This knowledge is an

37

added layer of protection for your business. The uniqueness of your business will dictate which is the best possible way to go.

Bank Loans

The American Hospital Association once used as its theme, "Get to know us before you need us." Ironic as it sounds, that advice applies also to doing business with a bank. The best time to talk to your banker is when you don't need money. It's obviously not true, as many people say, that banks only loan money to those who don't need it. But it is true that banks do not want to be loaning money to people and businesses that are not in a financial position to repay the amount borrowed. They only want to lend money to winners, not losers, and who can blame them?

The financial thrust of commercial bank loans is commercial and industrial short-term lending. Banks make money by buying and selling money. Making loans to customers is a primary source of bank income.[1] If you are going to need a business loan in the future, select the bank that you'd like to do business with. Then establish a relationship with a bank officer. Whether or not the bank promotes the concept of having a "personal banker," it is very desirable to have a decision maker at the bank get to know you on a personal level. Work at this relationship, so that the person knows and recognizes you. Introduce your banker to your franchisor. You can also use the knowledge and experience of your banker by placing her in an advisory position to your company.[2] Provide her with the franchise marketing brochure, and even your franchise offering circular. If the franchisor is a public company, provide a copy of the annual report. Open a checking or savings account. Don't overdraw your checking account. Maintain good, consistent growth in your savings accounts.

Know what it is you want to borrow money for. The bank will definitely ask you that question. Is it to start the business? If so, you'll need a detailed operating plan with budgets and cash flow projections. Is it to cover a working capital shortage? A bank might frown on this type of loan. This situation usually is covered best by a medium- to long-term capital infusion into the business. This may mean getting an outside investor. New equipment and facilities loans are often brought to bankers. You should project the increased profit projections as a result of this type of investment and how you will be able to pay back the loan through these increased profits. You'll have to substantiate these projections. This can be done with indications of increased orders from current customers, and new markets and how you'll penetrate those markets.

It is advisable to establish a solid credit rating, if you have not already accomplished this. Take out a small personal loan. Make prompt payments and, if possible, pay off the loan early. This can be done more than once. The result of this will be that the local credit bureau will have a good rating on you, and will reflect that you are a good credit risk. Be careful to keep all credit card accounts paid promptly, as well as any other loans and mortgage payments. All of this is reflected in your credit rating. This will be of great help when you are ready to apply for a business loan.

Also, start doing your homework. Find out what information your bank needs in order to consider giving you a business loan. When you make your request for credit, make it a presentation of your business plan, not a half-hearted, non-specific request for funds. Whatever you do, don't just drop off your loan application and hope for the best. You risk making a negative impression. Be prepared to discuss your business growth plans and your future relationship with that bank. Banks are looking for good customers for present and future relationships. They are likely to be interested in your plans, and in the growth and prosperity of your business.

You'll be going to the bank for a secured or unsecured loan, or a secured or unsecured line of credit. Secured means the loan is backed by collateral, which can be in the form of personal property or real estate. It is put in place to reduce risk to the lender. You, of course, must realize that if you cannot repay the loan, you are at risk of losing your collateral.

The following are some measures used by banks in evaluating your creditworthiness:

1. Quality of accounts receivable and inventory

2. Measure of business margins and ratios against industry standards

3. Quality of collateral

4. Quality and frequency of financial reporting

5. Years of profitability

6. Years in business

Be sure to note that the word "quality" is present very often. That's no accident. Now, what information will the bankers require in order to service your request?[3]

1. The banker will generally ask you to fill out a financial report.

2. If it is a corporation, a list of the assets and liabilities of the corporation, called a "balance sheet," will also be requested. The bankers will clearly want to review the current financial status of the business by means of the "balance sheet."

3. If there are a number of principals in the business, and especially if it is not a corporation, more than one of you will likely be asked to provide a financial statement (a complete disclosure of your personal assets and liabilities).

4. They also will ask for cash flow projections, and,

5. A statement as to how you plan to use this money in your business.

A business plan also should be available. A well-organized, carefully developed business plan can give fledgling management some guidelines in developing short- and long-range goals. It also can serve to unify your management into a team as you work together to meet those goals. It also will demonstrate to the banker that you have thought through the development of your business. Information from your franchisor will be of great value in the development of your business plan.

A Start-Up Business Plan

Business plans can vary for the start-up business, but there are some essentials that should be included in every plan.

1. A description of your company and the management capabilities of those in key management positions

2. Company goals and objectives

3. The proposed market for the business or service

4. How you plan to reach that proposed market

5. How you will use available marketing tools so you can achieve a significant share of the market

6. A business budget or financial plan for a one- to five-year period, including a detailed projection of earnings, along with all appropriate assumptions. I prefer a three-year projection with two to three scenarios, reflecting best-case and worst-case projections, along with a most likely scenario.

7. How much money is needed by the company

8. How and when that money will be paid back to the lender of the funds

9. The collateral that will be offered as security for the loan, along with the present market value of that security

10. Timetables of forecasts and future events

There is an excellent series of booklets available through the Small Business Administration on the subject of business plans with specific guides for retailers, service businesses, and manufacturers. They deal with developing marketing plans, determining sales potential, choosing a site, attracting customers, doing customer service profiles, developing sales techniques, determining company structure, and cash budgeting. There are also books available from the government that serve as guides to capital sources. If you have never taken the time to do a complete business plan, and feel that you do not have the financial ability to be assisted by a financial or business consultant, these booklets are excellent guides to take you through the necessary steps. Also, recently there have been computer software programs developed that are designed to walk you through the development of a business plan. Perhaps your franchisor will assist you. Just going through the motions of making a business plan can be beneficial to the principals in a business. The exercise gives you the opportunity to see your goals, objectives, tactics, and strategies clearly defined.

In targeting the needs of your business during the first year, include the amount of money you'll need to live on, as a business cost, in the form of a salary. Be sure it's realistic. Do an analysis of your life-style, and your fixed and variable costs. Be sure that you maintain necessary insurance policies. A family emergency, without insurance, could put you in a severe financial pinch and seriously infringe on your ability to run your business.

A Business Plan for Established Businesses

If your business is already established, the Business Plan should include:[4]

1. A profit and loss statement for the previous full year and for the current period to the date of the balance sheet

2. Balance sheet

3. Cash flow charting

4. Sales projections

5. A marketing plan

6. Inventory reports

7. A five-year growth projections plan

8. How you plan to pay this money back to the bank

9. The collateral to be offered (examples of collateral can be mortgage on land, a building and/or equipment, or securities you may hold)

10. Amount of loan and how it is to be used (it can be assignment of warehouse receipts for marketable merchandise or assignment of current receivables)

11. Current personal financial statements for each partner or stockholder owning 20 percent or more of the business

12. Tax reports for the past five years

Be aware of compensating balances. Banks often require that a percentage of your loan remain in the bank. If you are paying 12 percent interest for the total loan, and receiving 6 percent interest on the money that you cannot use, there is an added business cost that has to be applied to that loan. Be sure to take that into consideration when doing business with a bank.

Banks take a particularly cautious approach when lending money to small businesses, since a large percentage of these loans result in bankruptcy. As has been stated, a great number of small businesses never survive to their fifth anniversary, largely because of inadequate capitalization and poor management. Be sure that your bank is aware of the significantly better statistics for the business survival and longevity of franchises. Include this information in your business plan. It could help in your successful presentation for financing. Nevertheless, you do want to avoid inadequate capitalization. Having a well-developed business plan is essential. Even with a business plan, banks often will require that a loan for a small business be secured by personal and/or business assets; or have a financially secure person co-sign your note.

It is possible that even with excellent credit you may be turned down by a bank. An article in the November 1988 issue of Venture magazine[5] expressed concern that banks were backing off from financing new businesses due to their own problems. More recently, the March 3,1992, issue of the Rocky Mountain News[6] provided a feature stating that "small-business operators say bank credit has dried up." Banks were concerned about their own low profits. Many had overextended themselves, having made loans collateralized by real estate. The bust in real estate in various parts of the country followed by the recession in the early 1990s only aggravated this problem.

Private Capital

Some private companies, like Merrill, Lynch, Pierce, Fenner, & Smith, have loan programs available.[7] They have one type of particular importance to small business. It is called the Equity Access Credit Account. It is a source to be investigated, as the cost is reasonable, and they are responsive to the needs of businesses.

The largest single lender to franchisees is the Money Store. With offices throughout the U.S., they provide significant financing to start-up franchisees. These are usually loans secured by real estate. Another source of private funding is the Pacific Funding Group based in Irvine, California. Like the Money Store, they are an asset-based financier. They advertise that they will use the business assets as the primary source of capital. New private sources of franchise financing continue to develop, as franchising grows more significant in our economy.

A Line of Credit

It is often advisable to request a line of credit instead of a loan. If, for instance, you need $20,000 capital, but you don't need it in a lump sum, you could apply for a $20,000 line of credit. This would be especially true of retail and manufacturing businesses. With a $20,000 loan, you would have total use of those moneys, but you'd be paying interest on the total amount of the loan. If you negotiate a $20,000 line of credit with the banking institution, you can draw down the moneys as needed. Since the bills most likely will come in at different times, and since there is adequate cash flow on some merchandise, you may only be drawing down a part of the $20,000. The benefit to you in using a line of credit is that, should you need the total amount, it is available to you. But if you don't, you're only paying interest on the amount you need. That controls one cost to your business.

SBA Loans

If you have been turned down by a bank for a conventional loan, you may apply to the bank for a Small Business Administration (SBA) guaranteed loan.[8] Usually, only a few banks in your area make these loans. Most larger banking institutions do a relatively small percentage of their loan business through the SBA guaranteed loan program. Some bankers viewed these loans as higher-risk business loans, and have opted not to become involved in the program. However, new procedures have been introduced to encourage more financial institutions to become involved directly in these programs, and SBA representatives claim the red tape problem has been relieved.

The SBA has provided a wide range of loan programs available to those experiencing difficulty in securing conventional financing. They accomplish this by providing guarantees to lenders. The following are the SBA loan programs currently available.[9]

I. Guaranteed Loan Program

Guaranteed loans are made by private lenders and are guaranteed up to 90 percent by the SBA. There are three principal players in the SBA guaranteed loan—the SBA, the small business borrower, and the private lender. The major role is played by the lender, as it determines if the loan application submitted by the small business is acceptable. If it is, the lender forwards the application and its credit analysis to the SBA. After SBA approval, the lender disburses the funds. It is then up to the borrower to make appropriate payments to the lender.

Most SBA loans are made under the Guaranteed Loan Program.

2. Small Loan Program

To meet the need for loans of $50,000 or less, the SBA initiated the Small Loan Program. This type of loan would be of particular value to small firms in the service sector. To encourage use of the Small Loan Program, the SBA has changed the guarantee fee to participating lenders and simplified the application form.

3. 504 Certified Development Company Program

A 504 CDC loan provides long-term financing for acquiring land, buildings, machinery, and equipment and for building, modernizing, renovating, or restoring existing facilities and sites. Project size must be at least $125,000. An SBA 504 loan gives the small business owner the means to expand, modernize, and compete in the business world.

4. Export Revolving Line of Credit Program

The SBA's Export Revolving Line of Credit Program helps small businesses export their products or services. It is an unlikely source of debt capital for most franchisees.

5. Contract Loan Program

The Contract Loan Program is a short-term line of credit designed to finance the estimated costs of materials and labor needed to perform a specific contract. The loan is guaranteed by the SBA, but does not allow revolving account access to the funds guaranteed by the agency. Applicants must provide a specific product or service under an assignable contract. The amount can by up to $750,000 and may be guaranteed up to 85 percent.

6. Seasonal Line of Credit

The SBA Seasonal Line of Credit Program offers short-term loans to small businesses that are in a financial crunch due to seasonal changes in business volume. Applicants must establish a definite pattern of seasonal activity and cannot be eligible under the Contract Loan Program. The amount loaned can be up to $750,000 and may be guaranteed up to 85 percent.

7. Handicapped Assistance Loans

Handicapped individuals and public or private nonprofit organizations that employ handicapped persons and operate in their interest can acquire financing for the operation of a small business. Eligibility varies for individuals and organizations.

Certain food franchisors, such as Arby's, have initiated programs for employing the handicapped. Should you wish to implement such a program, you may be eligible for the funds made available through this program.

8. Veteran Programs

The SBA will secure business financing for Vietnam-era and disabled veterans who are unable to obtain a loan through the private sector. Veterans can use the loan to set up a small business. The ceiling on this type of loan is $150,000. Contact your local SBA office for eligibility. In addition, many franchisors will assist veterans under this program. Obtain an up-to-date list of these franchisees from the SBA.

9. Disaster Program

The SBA Disaster Program offers low-interest, long-term loans to help small businesses that are financially affected by a declared disaster. See Chapter 12 for more information regarding natural disasters and their potential impact on your business.

How to Apply for an SBA Loan[10]

If you decide to apply for an SBA guaranteed loan, the following are the procedures to be initiated:

1. Prepare a detailed and comprehensive business plan.

2. Prepare a current business balance sheet listing all assets, liabilities, and net worth. Applicants for business start-up loans should prepare an estimated balance sheet as of the day the business is to start. Be sure to include the amount that you and others will invest.

3. Prepare profit and loss statements for the current period and for the three most recent fiscal years. Business start-up applicants should prepare a detailed projection of earnings and expenses for at least the first year of operation. A monthly cash flow projection is recommended.

4. Prepare a personal financial statement of the proprietor and/or each partner and stockholder owning 20 percent or more of the corporate stock in the business.

5. List collateral to be offered as security for the loan. Include present market value and any existing liens on the collateral.

6. State the amount of the loan requested and the purposes for which it is to be used.

7. Take this to your lender. If the lender is unwilling to provide the financing, explore the possibility of an SBA guaranteed loan with the lender or contact your local SBA office.

8. If you have exhausted the possibility of private financing or even an SBA guaranteed loan, you may be eligible for an SBA direct loan, depending on the availability of funds.

SBA Programs for Women and Minorities

The SBA does not consider women to be a disadvantaged minority. There are no specific financing programs for women-owned businesses, however the SBA is well aware of the growth of women-owned businesses and has a number of programs that are available to all small businesses and others that can specifically help women-owned businesses. They are as follows:

I. The Office of Women's Business Ownership

Recognizing the growth of women-owned businesses, this office is available to help women gain access to the federal marketplace. They will help you to become aware of long-term training and counseling opportunities. The sole purpose of this office is to help women entrepreneurs.

2. Women's Network for Entrepreneurial Training (WNET)

WNET provides a special mentoring program. It has been operating successfully for years. This agency seeks to network emerging entrepreneurs with successful women chief executive officers (CEOs).

3. Procurement Automated Source System (PASS)

The PASS program is designed to profile your company and to make that information available to government agencies and to major corporations. This can assist in the growth of your business. This program does not guarantee solicitations, but it does increase your business exposure.

4. 8(a) Program

If you are an American citizen and open at least 51 percent of a business and belong to one of the groups of individuals who have been determined to be socially and economically disadvantaged and have had difficulty entering the mainstream, you may be eligible for participation in the 8(a) contracting program. Socially disadvantaged refers specifically to those who have been subjected to racial, ethnic, or group prejudice. This program is considered to be the prime source of aid to minorities. Again, check with the local office of the SBA to determine if you are eligible.

Other SBA and Local Assistance

SBA also can help small firms that want to bid on government contracts and private sector contracts by helping them get the necessary bonding that might not ordinarily be available. Bonding is a form of insurance that is often required by certain businesses. If your business is too small or too young to qualify for bonding, the SBA can help you under certain circumstances, and has fact sheets dealing with the necessary information on getting bonding assistance.

Today, every state has a Small Business Development Corporation that has been organized to stimulate business and employment. Each one relies heavily on government loan guarantees, and is in a position to grant many loans that commercial banks deny. Remember that these programs change. They depend on the state of the local economy, the philosophy of the local legislature, and political and social pressures. Check with your state government to see if such a Development Corporation exists in your state.

In addition to the SBA, some states, like Mississippi, offer guaranteed loan programs geared specifically to small businesses. Others, including Maryland, offer special lending to minority-owned businesses. The state of New Jersey has started the New Jersey Economic Development Authority (NJEDA). The agency's impact, as presented in a February 10, 1992, article in *Crain's New York*, points to 73 projects started, more than $253 million invested in economic development resulting in 1,641 permanent jobs and 4,500 construction jobs.[11]

It is often very desirable to access local programs. For example, in 1989, Denver, Minneapolis, Seattle, Albuquerque, and Detroit, in cooperation with the SBA, made a special program available to businesswomen. Grants were be given in the form of counseling and management training. It is up to you to seek out this information. There is money out there. Although the governmental lending programs are fluid and thereby subject to change, if your business needs capital, and qualifies, the following are potential sources for that capital.

Employee Stock Option Plan (ESOP)

Under U.S. Law, an employee stock option plan (ESOP) can both provide immediate cash to a small business and create a retirement benefit for the firm's employees. The business issues stock that has previously been unissued and contributes it to an employee retirement fund. The contribution is tax deductible. The benefit is that the deduction can be carried back against income in more profitable years to create immediate tax reimbursement. This provides new capital for your business, as well as substantial retirement benefits to your employees. There are human resource benefits to be reaped with an ESOP, because your employees now have a direct stake in the success of your business.

Credit Unions

Another source of capital, available to only a limited few, is from credit unions. One must belong to a credit union in order to take advantage of their services. The basis for a credit union resides in a unifying characteristic of the credit union members. Sometimes employees of a company have a credit union, such as United Airlines credit union. Other times, a labor union has a credit union. In other situations, a social organization, such as a women's business group, or a church group, can be the basis of such an organization. Whatever it is, if you are a member, check the requirements for taking a loan from the credit union. Sometimes, moneys can be available on very competitive and favorable terms to members.

Insurance Policies

Should you be fortunate enough to have established an insurance policy that provides an accumulating cash value, you could consider borrowing from your policy (at what often can be a very favorable rate) as a way to finance a new franchise or expand your current business.

Venture Capital

Venture capital[12] companies are in the business of investing money in return for an equity position in the company. Venture capital is especially suited for the firm that cannot raise moneys in the more traditional money markets. Borrowers turn to venture capitalists when they are looking for the opportunity to give their companies a higher rate of growth than might ordinarily be possible. Venture capitalists specialize in high-growth, high-risk, newer companies, and potentially high-return investments. For their capital, you can expect to give up a portion of the ownership of your business. There is a substantial risk in this, because if the growth and development program do not work out as expected, there is the possibility of losing control of one's own business. A traditional, single-unit franchisee is highly unlikely to qualify for funds from a venture capitalist. However, franchise area development agreements targeting large territories, major growth, and high potential returns could qualify for venture capital.

It's likely that the venture capitalist firm will have a representative on your board of directors, but it's unlikely they will be involved in the day-to-day operations of the firm. Their participation on the board can be very beneficial, though, since venture capitalists are likely to have sophisticated and sound business sense, and excellent business contacts.

There is a generally accepted formula of ownership by the venture capital firm, but you really should try to negotiate the percentage. If the venture capital firm enters during what is considered to be the high-risk stage, where the company is being established, 40 to 50 percent ownership is considered acceptable. If it comes in after the business is already established, but not yet profitable, 35 to 40 percent is common practice. If the venture capital firm enters when the business is established and beginning to be profitable, a 25 to 30 percent ownership would be acceptable. If your business is profitable, and you believe that a substantial infusion of capital will cause a burst of growth, this might be an appropriate capital source.

The venture capital firm can provide the money and the guidance for capital growth, bridge financing, recapitalization of the business, and other services, including leveraged buyouts. Minimum loans are approximately $500,000 and can go up into the millions of dollars. Typical investments are in the $500,000 to $1 million range.

Many venture capital firms have been organized under the Small Business Investment Act of 1958.[13] These are known as SBICs (Small Business Investment Companies) and include those that are owned or controlled by commercial banks, those that are publicly held, those that are privately held, and those that are subsidiaries of operating companies. Many are private firms, which are structured as partnerships and corporations and are backed by institutional investors such as insurance firms, banks, and trust departments. Others are family owned and operated. Still others are divisions of large corporations that have been formed with the long-range intent of creating merger and acquisition opportunities. All have been licensed by the Small Business Administration to work with entrepreneurs. SBICs must follow the Small Business Administration's definition of a small business, which primarily means businesses of under 100 employees. This includes virtually all franchises. What is important is that although an SBIC can own stock in your company, it cannot own the controlling interest.

When approaching a venture capital firm, you will need:

1. A complete business plan

2. Resumes of those employees who are important to the success of the business

3. An analysis of present and potential competitors, principal suppliers, and customers

4. An analysis of the strengths and weaknesses of the business venture

5. Marketing data that are substantive and supportable

6. Current financials, along with the historical data supporting growth

Venture capitalists are going to want an exit clause in the agreement, since their purpose is not to stay with the business venture over the long haul. They want their profit at some point, and want to have those moneys to invest in new ventures. The way it's done should be agreed upon before the loan is accepted. There are four common ways that the exit is accomplished:

1. A public offering by the venture capitalists of their share in the company;

2. The same public offering, but including some of the entrepreneur's stock at the time of the public offering;

3. A merger or acquisition by another company; or

4. The repurchase by the entrepreneur of the investor's share in his/her company.

In seeking out a loan from a venture capitalist, remember that many of these firms may have developed expertise in certain areas such as real estate, retailing, medical devices, and may tend to specialize by loaning primarily to businesses in these areas. Recognize this, and you will save a great deal of time by approaching the firm most likely to invest in your business.

An excellent source guide to venture capitalists is Pratt's Guide to Venture Capital Sources, published annually by Pratt & Morris.

Trade Credit

In a few rare cases, you can borrow from the franchisor. It is not often an option, but occasionally a franchisor will finance part of the franchise fee or certain merchandise. Be sure to ask. The information is always available in the offering circular, so you can check that first.

In certain situations, businesses can even borrow from their suppliers. This is not general practice, but is possible in certain industries. It can actually amount to a negotiated, no-interest loan to your business. It can greatly enhance your cash flow position as well as reduce or eliminate at least one substantial business cost.

Borrowing inventory and other supplies is also possible. An example could be distributors and publishers. Publishers cannot stay in business without bookstores and outlets. Should your distributor be caught with an oversupply or a storage problem, deals sometimes can be worked out in favor of the bookstore or outlet. You might be able to arrange to get your inventory on consignment, or with a three- to six-month payback provision. If you could turn your inventory during that time period, you could (in one very real sense) be using your supplier as a source of credit. You would, in effect, have inventory without a large investment. The trick is in being able to turn that inventory in time to pay for the merchandise according to your agreement, to maximize cash flow.

There are businesses where consignment purchases, or longer-than-usual payback provisions, are negotiable. It is essential that you, as a successful businessperson, evaluate your franchise business area to see if this is a possibility. The possibility also could exist in industries where there is heavy competition among suppliers. In that case, special terms might be established so a supplier could secure your account.

Funding by Leasing

Equipment leasing traditionally has been a strong source of funding for franchisees. In the food and automotive areas, a good deal of equipment has been acquired through leasing. Those investing in higher-tech equipment, such as printing franchisees, would be wise to consider leasing. Rapid technology changes dictate updated equipment in order to remain competitive. Leasing permits continued access to new, technologically improved equipment.

Some of the specific advantages of leasing are:[14]

1. No down payment or a very small outlay of first and last month payments

2. Conservation of capital. Remember capital is usually a very limited resource in growing businesses

3. Lower costs through tax benefits. When the tax benefits go to the leasing company, this usually is reflected in lower costs to the lessee

4. Fully deductible payments as an operating expense

5. Lower risk of equipment obsolescence

6. Longer term than loans

7. Flexible payment schedule

8. Preservation of credit capacity

9. Lower present value costs. Present value is the concept used to measure the worth of a sum of money to be received in the future in terms of today's dollars. This takes into account the growth value of the money.

Disadvantages of Leasing[15]

1. No equity buildup in the equipment

2. Higher costs than buying

3. Long-term debt

4. No termination without penalty

5. Contractual limitations. For example, the equipment is always owned by the lessor and must be maintained in a specific manner

6. Transaction costs, such as added legal and accounting analysis, due to the complexity of leasing contracts

One important growing area in franchising is that of mobile-based franchises. All kinds of franchises from Express Lube, Dr. Vinyl, Pressed 4 Time, Wash on Wheels, and the Glass Doctor all deliver their varied services by van. Franchisees that ordinarily might have difficulty getting a loan for a new business can frequently get the basic unit of equipment for their mobile-based business—a fully equipped van—financed by means of leasing. This allows many new franchisees to access necessary start-up capital. It's definitely an area to be considered for many businesses.

Saving Money on Taxes

High-quality tax advice can help you minimize your tax burden and keep your capital in your franchised business. Acquiring the services of the best qualified tax accountant you can afford can be the best investment your business will make. Your accountant can direct you in deferring taxes, taking tax investment credits and depreciation benefits, and keep you up to date on new tax laws. For instance, should you decide to take a second mortgage on your home, it can be tax deductible. You have to have the right information in order to make the right decisions. Good tax advice can be a great financial benefit to your company.

It is also important to work with an accountant who follows the status of new bills and proposals before the U.S. Congress. Should some of these become law, immediate business decisions could result in an improved cash position for small business.

Initial Public Offerings

For the single-unit franchise, issuing stock via a public offering[16] is generally an unrealistic way to raise capital. However, it is a possibility when we consider area development agreements of capital-intensive businesses. For instance, there have been public offerings of companies that have the developmental rights to a certain franchise, such as McDonald's, or companies that own the rights to three or more fast-food franchises in a particular market.

When interest rates are high, making a loan prohibitive, and when a growing franchise has a good track record and good management, the best step may be for the company to go public. However, the drawback to this is that it encompasses traditionally high legal and accounting fees. Trying to go public without the assistance of these specialists is to expose yourself to high risks because complete disclosure of your company's strengths and weaknesses is dictated by law. Also, to do it yourself is to take the added risk that your stock may not sell, leaving you with high costs and an unsuccessful public offering. That combination could lead to the demise of your business. For this reason you will require the backing of a sound underwriter who is familiar with the Initial Public Offering (IPO) market and who has a successful track record. A risk to be considered is that you could lose control of your company if more than 51 percent of the stock is offered on the public market. (The theory behind this is that it takes less than 50 percent to control a publicly held company. Even though that is generally true, it isn't necessarily true if stock distribution is not broad-based.)

There is now a simpler way to go public. That is to buy a public shell or a blind pool. A public shell is a public corporation without an active business source. The business may have gone bankrupt or sold its assets. A blind pool is a public shell sold to speculative buyers on the premise that it will be merged with an active business. As soon as you merge with a public shell or blind pool, you become a public company. You can then establish market relationships and sell stock to raise additional capital. The shell or blind pool may even have warrants in place for this purpose. A good source for these public shells or blind pools is in the business opportunity classified advertising section of *The Wall Street Journal*.

Assistance from Local Government

There is also the possibility of local governmental assistance in the form of industrial revenue bonds—tax-free bonds issued and guaranteed by a community. The advantage to these is that you can borrow the money at substantially lower interest rates than those available elsewhere. What the community gets in return is the advantage of having your business provide jobs and a stronger tax base in the community.

Other forms of governmental assistance include loans (available from several states), direct equity financing (available in Connecticut), and working capital loans (available in California and Colorado). Check with the state department of corporations or the appropriate corporate regulatory authority in your state to find out what local and state assistance is available to community business-persons.

Investment Money from Partners

One also can consider taking in a partner to provide needed capital:

- *A silent partner:* He would put up some money and achieve partial ownership, but not be involved in the day-to-day management of the business.

- *A limited partner:* He would have limited liability, no decision-making powers, and certain tax advantages.

- *A general partner:* He would be actively involved in the management.

- *A unique partnership:* There are occasionally very creative partnerships that are developed. One such example is that of the National Association of Negro Professional and Business Women's Club (NAPBWC). The two groups entered into joint venture partnership with American Speedy Printing Centers in order to help finance some members of their organization, and thereby permit them to start franchises.

If a partnership looks attractive to you, you'll have to evaluate the benefits and drawbacks such a relationship would bring to your business. If, for instance, you wanted to buy a travel agency franchise, and your partner had management skills while you had the skills of marketing travel services, such a partnership could be mutually beneficial. With better capital positioning and complementary business skills, the partnership could contribute greatly to the success of the business. Note: There also have been breakups of partnerships that resemble the crumbling of a marriage, causing the business to suffer and sometimes even fail. When I am working with clients considering a partnership, I have a general recommendation. Plan to invest in at least two units of the particular franchise. Buy one and take an option on another. Once established, open the second unit. This way, if you are not getting along, each party can take one unit, and part in a reasonably content manner.

Borrowing Money from Relatives

Borrowing money from relatives is a common way for small business owners to get their companies financed. However it must be handled as a business, not as a family matter. A business plan should be developed, focusing on the same elements as any other business plan, but particularly on how and when the moneys will be paid back to the lender.

1. Will the lender earn a percentage of the ownership?

2. Will the lender get interest on his moneys?

3. Will the interest float with current interest rates?

Handling a loan from relatives in a businesslike manner can help to reopen that door in the future if moneys are again needed. Your family also will have increased respect for your business ability and in your business. It will also go a long way in ensuring harmonious relationships in both the business and the family. Should the negotiations be casual the business have payback problems with no arrangements for such contingencies, emotional and family upheaval could cause your business to fail. This scenario is regrettable, since it is avoidable.

Just Plain Creativity

Sometimes creativity can help with cash flow, too. For example, the November 1991 issue of *Entrepreneur*[17] featured a delicatessen owner who resolved a short-term cash flow problem by selling "Deli Dollars." People paid $9 for $10 in coupons. Of course, as a franchisee, this type of program would require franchisor approval. It could also be the basis of a promotion for you and your fellow franchisees.

Corporate Barter

Perhaps the most creative practice is corporate barter. I talked with Liz Scherr, franchisee for the office of Itex of Denver. Itex is the largest retail barter exchange in the country. The Denver office coordinates some 350 merchants in the exchange of their goods and services. Don't be mistaken and think this is some small operation. A merchant can barter her goods and services and have access to a very large array of services. These include accountants, lawyers, advertising, art galleries, and all kinds of auto services, including auto brokers. Bartering also encompasses restaurant meals, business machinery servicing, contractors of all types, hotel rooms for business and vacation, and business and marketing consultants. There is a small fee to join an Itex office. In addition, one pays a 10 percent cash fee to the franchisee. The 10 percent is the franchisee's source of income. When considering creative sources of capital for your business, barter should be placed high on the list. You could start the day with breakfast in a restaurant, follow up by contracting the services of a computer programmer, and then end the day with a relaxing massage. It's all available by means of barter.

Most businesses require a dependable source of capital since peaks and valleys are encountered during their business cycle. Understanding these business cycles, and preparing for them by establishing a sound loan relationship with a financial institution, can spell the difference between the success and failure of a business. Inadequate capitalization is often given as one of the prime reasons businesses fail. Franchises are no exception. This is avoidable with proper planning. These suggestions should help you to broaden your ideas on where and how to get business capital, and to establish new and productive future sources of capital for your business.

ENDNOTES

[1] *Doing Business With Banks*, Gibson Heath, United Banks of Colorado, Inc., Denver, CO, 1989.

[2] Ibid.

[3] Ibid.

[4] James G. Simmons, *Creative Business Financing*, Prentice-Hall, Inc., Englewood Cliffs, NJ, 1982.

[5] "Banks are Backing Off From Venture Capital Management," *Venture*, New York, NY, November 1988, p. 26.

[6] "Small Business Operators Say Bank Credit has Dried Up," *Rocky Mountain News*, Denver, CO, March 3, 1992.

[7] "The Flexible Credit Account," Merrill Lynch, New York, NY, 1988.

[8] James B. Black, Jr., *SBA Loans, Jian Tools for Sales, Inc.*, SBA, 1991.

[9] *The Building Blocks to Small Business Success*, September 18, 1992, The U.S. Small Business Administration, SBA Authorization #88-1287, Fargo, ND.

[10] Ibid.

[11] "Hint of Revival: SBA Lending Surges in New York," *Crain's New York*, New York, NY, February 10–16, 1992.

[12] *Raising Venture Capital, An Entrepreneur's Guidebook*, Deloitte Haskins Sells, 1982.

[13] *Doing Business With Banks*, Gibson Heath, United Banks of Colorado, Inc., Denver, CO, 1989.

[14] *Small Business Reporter, Equipment Leasing*, published by Bank of America, produced by Marketing Publications, San Francisco, CA, 1982.

[15] Ibid.

[16] *Strategies For Going Public, An Entrepreneur's Guidebook*, Deloitte Haskins Sells, 1983.

[17] "Trading Up," *Entrepreneur*, New York, NY, November 1991.

PART TWO

Reach Your Target Market

CHAPTER 4

Analyzing Competition in the 1990s

Competition is a key element in a capitalistic society. When you go into business, or expand your current business, it is absolutely necessary to analyze the competition. This analysis is also a vital part of an ongoing business plan. We're not talking about a theoretical analysis of the competition; we are referring to the practical elements that you should evaluate so that your franchised business can thrive in the competitive marketplace.

In franchising you have a three-tier evaluation of competitors:

1. Competitive franchisees in your market

2. Competitive franchisors

3. Independents

It is unlikely that you as a single independent franchisee will be in a financial position to conduct a thorough evaluation of the competition without assistance from your franchisor. However, franchisees, in cooperation with their franchisor, can initiate a valuable competitive analysis.

The first step is to identify the competitive franchisors, as well as strong national and regional independents. Then, unit franchisees or groups of franchisees in a particular market could identify those they believe are the strong independent competitors in their particular market.

Together the group could set objectives for the information that would be gathered to give them a competitive advantage. The following is a list of some of the useful information that needs to be accumulated in respect to franchisor competitors (and a similar list should be drawn up for major independents operating in your marketplace):

1. Market share of competitors

2. Target market of competitors

3. Stated and unstated financial goals of franchisor. What competitive tradeoffs does the competitor make? For example, do they appear to focus on long-term or short-term strategies?[1] This information would contribute to the development of competitive strategy.

4. Can you determine their attitude toward risk? Do they appear risk-averse or aggressive in terms of expansion?[2]

5. Does the organization have economic or non-economic values? Are these shared among senior management? Do they wish to have major market share? Do they want to add only 10-12 new franchises per year? Do they wish to expand regionally? nationally? internationally?

5. Are they well capitalized?

6. Have you evaluated the quality and cohesiveness of their management team?

7. Do they have a strong advisory team?

8. What are their weaknesses?

9. Is there harmony among their franchisees?

10. Are you in a position to take advantage of these weaknesses?

A program I participated in provides a good example of how franchisees and franchisors can draw up a plan of competitive action. At one point, Weight Watchers decided to develop a new eating program to address changes in the marketplace as well as competition. I chaired a committee of 12 Weight Watchers franchisees with the explicit task of developing a new eating plan. After countless meetings held across the country, we presented the plan to the staff of dietitians working for Weight Watchers International. Cooperatively, we finalized the details of the program. Simultaneously, a committee of franchisees, marketing executives of Weight Watchers International, and professionals from the independent advertising and public relations companies on contract to Weight Watchers International developed the marketing approach to be taken in the introduction of this new eating plan. The cooperation and synergy resulted in an exciting and very successful expansion of the business.

Staying on Top of Competition

One major bank holding company had an advertising campaign in which they announced, "To truly become #1 you must constantly strive to surpass yourself, not the competition." Impressive slogan, but in reality, we do have to understand our competitors and what the effects of competition are. Keep in mind that understanding the competition allows the franchisor to develop a strategic niche. The aim would be to make this a particularly profitable niche. The following are some additional incentives for better understanding your competitors:

1. Competition can keep you on your toes, so that you constantly ensure that your business is run effectively and efficiently.

2. Competition can cause hardships to your business by forcing you to expand or to grow faster than you're capable of.

3. Competition can help create an atmosphere that permits consumers to seek out a centralized locale for a particular item. For example, you will find a section for shoe shops in many malls. You will also find neighborhoods with many furniture stores.

4. Competition can diminish your share of the marketplace, or it can also expand and increase the general market for the product or service.

5. Competition can hurt one business while it benefits another.

How effectively you react to competition in your chosen field and locale will determine the success of your business. Understanding that competition can be both friend and foe can help you in developing business policies to insure that you outlive your competition.

Understanding Your Competition

You should be looking at the competition that exists in the marketplace, and at the nature of that competition. You can start by reviewing the Franchise 500 in the January issue of *Entrepreneur Magazine* or the Franchise Opportunities Handbook. However, it is important to expand the concept of competition from a very narrow one, that of the same type of product or service, to include any business—franchise or not—that competes for the same dollars in your particular marketplace. There are currently over 35 print franchises. There are more than 20 shipping and packaging franchises.[3] When is enough enough or too much? Ask yourselves these questions:

1. If your franchisor has a patent or trademark on a particular product, does that guarantee your position in that market?

2. Do other products do basically the same job?

3. Are they cheaper?

4. Are these products more easily obtainable?

5. Is it easier to get parts and to repair them?

6. What kinds of skills are required to use the product?

7. Is there a higher degree of specialization required to operate your product?

8. Can the service be readily duplicated?

9. Is the competitor's delivery time the same as yours?

These are some of the questions that potential customers will be asking, and that you'll need to ask about yourself and your competition. You'll want to know that your own franchisor is on top of these questions and understands the importance of getting answers. Is the franchisor doing research and development, assuring that its franchisees are marketing competitive, up-to-date products and services in the most successful manner? The real world of competition is a pragmatic and fluctuating one. Understanding your competition gives you the necessary tools to develop superior products and services, increasing your chances for success in a competitive environment.

There may be a great deal of competition to analyze within your business area. Look at weight reduction franchisors. Weight Watchers, The Diet Center, Nutri-System, Jenny Craig, Physicians Weight Loss Centers, and more. Even franchising gets crowded with competitors, each approaching the market in its own way. Weight Watchers once had the field to itself. Today it is continually losing market share to competitors. Once the leader, it appears today to be the follower. Once the creative advertiser, today it appears to primarily offer discounting to attract clientele.

Identifying the Range of Competition

Sometimes there are many buyers and sellers in a marketplace. There is also the possibility of only one seller and many buyers. An example of this would be a utility that has been given the sole franchise to do business in a particular geographical area. This is referred to as a monopoly.

At other times there is only one buyer and many sellers. An example of this situation is a large textile plant established in an isolated area, which is the principal employer and purchaser of products in that area. Although the company is not a direct competitor, their salary levels could affect the salary levels of your employees.

Or, you may be the owner of a gift store franchise. A few miles down the road a major developer puts in a group of factory outlet stores. Now, you may find yourself competing with the manufacturer. You'd have the choice of selling at a lower price or changing your merchandise. As a franchisee that could be difficult. The example of clustered factory outlet stores throughout the nation proves that you now are vulnerable to this type of major competitive change.

Your evaluation should extend beyond your own community or neighborhood. You may find that your competition is many states away from your business operation, but still as effective as if they were right next door. That idea may initially appear farfetched to you, but after reading this chapter, you may decide otherwise.

One example of a far-away competitor might be in the video rental business. Perhaps you own the only video rental business in your community, giving you a monopoly of sorts for your particular locale. However, an analysis may show that many of the people in your community travel down a particular highway en route to a large shopping area, or on their way to work. That shopping area may be the site of a Blockbuster-type franchised video store. Perhaps the competitor is even geared to aggressively market and discount its prices. Now you ask, do you really have a neighborhood monopoly? Obviously not! There is aggressive competition for your customer dollars from another source.

Here is another possibility. Consider that you may have the only franchised stationery store in your community or neighborhood. Again, are you confident that you have some market control? You've done an analysis and discovered it is not worthwhile for another stationery store to open, since there's not adequate business for two similar stores. You are satisfied that people aren't traveling to the next community to shop for their needs.

Don't stop there in your market analysis. There are other factors you need to evaluate in today's highly technological marketplace. Can a businessperson in a neighboring community or another state contact your potential customers by telephone or through a mail order catalog? Office furniture, machinery, equipment, and supplies all are being marketed extensively by mail order catalogs today. Have you tuned into national cable networks that may be advertising specials to your customer base? These are common practices in today's highly competitive and dynamic business community. The customer who once depended on community businesses services now has access to the world of business via computers, cable television, fax, and phone.

How can you combat this competition? Do you offer better prices? Faster service? Delivery to the customer's office? Personalized service? Quick exchange for defective merchandise? Repair services? Do you offer fax services? Today, innovative restaurants are taking advance and delivery orders by fax, as are countless other types of businesses. Denver, Colorado, entrepreneur Rod Cyr organized Tasty Taxi, a food delivery business. His company picks up food from established restaurants and delivers it to individuals. Now he's franchising this business.

You cannot afford to be smug about competitive factors even when you appear to dominate a market. Competition isn't always visible. If it sufficiently erodes your business base, your business could fail. Awareness of all competitive factors is essential, so you can continue to be the major player in your field.

Team Up with Franchisor

Franchisees working together with their franchisor have attacked the issue of competition. According to Tricia Sheriff, president of the Foliage Design Systems Franchisee Advisory Council, their organization targeted new business development as the best way to gain an edge on competition. They identified a specific market niche, that of short-term events such as weddings and banquets. Together, franchisee and franchisor formed a plan to address this market.

Don Wollan, owner of four San Diego-based Burger King franchises, installed a soft foam playground that resulted in a 40 percent increase in family business. Not only did he install this playground equipment, but after shopping competitors, he installed a two-story version, more impressive than anything any other business in the neighborhood was offering.

It's essential that you as a franchisee take the initiative in gaining the marketing edge in your specific community. You—not your franchisor—have to continually analyze your business neighborhood to ensure continued dominance in your local marketplace. You'll frequently need franchisor approval for certain innovations, but you, like Don Wollan, can take the initial steps in bringing about innovation to your franchise.

Technological Change and Product Development

Technology and new product development also must be considered. Today, there is more computer technology available at lower prices, more efficient transportation, and better and different communication technology. These have all increasingly become part of our business and personal lives. As each day and year go by, our ways of doing business will continue to change. Traditional business boundaries will disappear.

Arby's has replaced employees by allowing customers to self-order by computer. There are drive-up fast food franchises, donut shops, photo centers, and more. A new franchise based in Littleton, Colorado, called The 4-SALE Hotline, is a residential real estate information service based on audio text technology. This technology is most familiar to us in the use of information systems. For instance, you call the Secretary of State's office in order to get information. You're told to press #1 for the office of business forms, #2 for corporate reports, and so on. Sometimes, you're given an option to speak to a person.

Another example of change that directly involves franchising is the sale of skin-care and cosmetic products. Upscale beauty products traditionally have been sold in department stores and beauty shops. Then along comes Merle Norman cosmetics and successfully sets up franchises in malls. These are shops that only sell the comprehensive line of Merle Norman cosmetics, and they offer consultation services. They provide skin analysis and make-up demonstrations.

Another successful new franchise to hit the U.S. market is an import from England, The Body Shop. This company only sells environmentally safe, natural skin-care products in their own shops in upscale malls. Known for attractive packaging, lovely fragrances, and attentive personnel, they have carved out a niche in the market.

These franchisors have introduced innovative ways to market skin-care products and cosmetics.

Consider Mobile-Based Franchises

A trend to look at is the proliferation of mobile-based franchises. Technological advances have encouraged the development of equipment that is small yet powerful. Franchises such as Pressed 4 Time, providing commercial dry cleaning delivery, Glass Doctor, providing glass repair by van, and Dr. Vinyl, providing vinyl and leather repair by van, are new ideas in delivery services.

Typically, mobile-based franchises provide low start-up costs as well as low overhead operations. In addition—and a very important addition—they often can get financing when other new businesses cannot. The banks are ready and willing to loan against a van as collateral, whereas in the current economic climate, banks generally appear risk-averse when it comes to new business loans. This change in the delivery of services directly affects real estate-bound businesses like dry cleaners, lube service centers, and fixed location glass repair services, along with any other businesses that have high real estate costs. Current franchises such as Grease Monkey, Jiffy Lube, Dry-Clean USA, and others will have to keep their eye on this new form of competition.

Application of Analysis

It's important to analyze successes and failures of competitors in the same and similar business fields, and then to apply this information to your own franchise. The following are some key applications:

1. Narrow the demographics of your target market

2. Improve site selection techniques

3. Improve media selection

4. Better allocate resources

5. Capitalize more on competitive weaknesses

6. Develop new products and services where there are voids in the market

Use this information and apply it to your business. Is there something they did that you should be doing or should be avoiding? You don't want to repeat someone else's errors, and you could benefit greatly from their successes, their original marketing ideas, and their innovative services.

An example of this is the apparent oversupply of yogurt shops. There are 10 yogurt franchises in the country. Yet it is easy for ice cream shops to compete by simply adding a yogurt machine, and that's what happened. Dairy Queen, major international franchisor, added yogurt to its product line and instantly became a major competitor. Many other franchisors did the same, as did supermarkets and independents. Overnight, the competitive marketplace changed dramatically for the yogurt franchisees.

Product Duplication

Another important area to analyze is, how easily can the product or service be duplicated? This could be a key question in your evaluation of future competitive factors and a major factor in the development of your business plan right now. If you are interested in buying a business or franchise, even one with a territorial guarantee, find out if there is a competitor readily able to duplicate your product or service. Then you must ask, how secure, really, is your position?

Let's say you are going to buy or already own a "Speedy X" printing franchise, which guarantees your territory for five square miles. You buy in and establish your business, only to have another printing franchise, "Speedy Z," open up across the street. That's certainly something you hadn't planned on. Perhaps there is adequate business for both of you, perhaps not. The same could hold true for "Burger Business A" and "Burger Business B," and for many other kinds of businesses. However, it's important to remember that the business owner with the greatest management skill base is the one most likely to survive adverse conditions and succeed in a competitive environment. Even as a franchisee, you cannot have all the bases covered. But you can try to plan ahead, to leave as little as possible to chance. Make sure the odds always are tilted in your favor.

Remember to maintain your perspective when it comes to competition. There are times when immediate competition is extremely healthy for a business. We're going to discuss these instances, too. Don't become paralyzed at the mere thought of competition. It's just essential to be aware and prepared so you can give yourself the best chance of being successful in your business.

Market Oversaturation

A good example of oversaturation of markets has been in the seminar business. At first it was only a few college professors and business consultants who were in the business of putting on seminars. Then new and more popular subjects evolved, and before long many people jumped on the seminar bandwagon. Some of them are good—professionals who have put much hard work and research into their presentations. Others are just trying to cash in on a big money maker and have little new to say. In the next few years, competition will bring about survival of the fittest. Meanwhile, an oversaturated field is rough on all of the participants.

Another example of oversaturation was the overnight appearance of plant and garden stores. Having living plants in your home took hold in the 1970s; it was fashionable. Before long, many a street corner sported a garden and floral shop, as it was a relatively easy concept to copy. However, it rapidly became a saturated market. Demand was soon satisfied, and the only ones that survived were those that practiced efficient business techniques. Then, another competitive dimension developed. Large food chains and department stores opened garden and floral departments. Their competitive edge was that they could appeal to large numbers of impulse shoppers. Soon after, many more neighborhood floral shops closed their doors. Today these businesses face new challenges. Technological research has resulted in the development of silk plants that look real. Franchisors such as Silk Plants, Etc. have taken up the call, and have challenged the current establishment.

Be especially careful of businesses that are very easy to get into, and initially appear to have high profit margins. Easy to get into simply means a business that doesn't require a specific set of skills or training. There are many other entrepreneurs looking for the same kinds of businesses. That's no reason to completely avoid these businesses. However, you do need to know that you'll likely be in a highly competitive atmosphere, and you'll need a marketing edge to succeed in that particular business. Franchising can be that edge. You may find that by associating with a franchise that has developed sophisticated marketing techniques, you will be best able to succeed in the oversaturated market. Franchising is specifically in place to help the independent with the more developed and advanced marketing techniques of larger businesses. You also will have to be assured of adequate capitalization so that you can be one of those who survive. Again, franchising, with its predictable analysis of capital requirements, can make the difference.

Market Specialization

In your analysis of the marketplace, you should determine how specialized you want your business or service to be. Concentrate on those markets where you have a distinct advantage, both geographically and in terms of product line. By doing this, and by segmenting the market, you may find the key to business success in today's highly competitive business climate. High interest and marketing costs, limited resources, and limited distribution outlets are all factors that make marketing segmentation more appealing.

In targeting the best market for your product or service, you may need to consider the age, sex, education level, income level, ethnic background, religious background, home owners versus renters, geographical segmentation, and other characteristics of your potential customers. Carefully evaluating the market segment you intend to develop for your product or service is beneficial. Some examples are a "nearly-new" resale shop, an Hispanic radio or TV station, an exclusive boutique, or a "faux" jewelry shop. One woman opened a "nearly-new" shop in a college community and, since it was directed to the right clientele, her business was successful. Another woman saw the lack of availability of Spanish language books in her community—which had a 23 percent Spanish surnamed population— and she opened an Hispanic bookstore to fill the need. A father and son's family-oriented jewelry store expanded their service to include items children could buy for their parents, and a very popular jewelry repair service. These businesses were based on the principles of marketing segmentation.

Marketing segmentation theory states that if you have a market segment or niche that is unserved, or perceives itself to be unserved or underserved, then a business that develops a product or service for that marketplace can succeed. In addition, correct placement of one's business in the marketplace is an effective means of competition.

For example, during the 1970s, women felt excluded from the financial world and were often intimidated by financial institutions. Yet they were becoming more financially independent and financially sophisticated. They were ready for a bank of their own. Marketing performed for the organizers of the Women's Bank in Denver, Colorado, by an independent marketing firm demonstrated that there was a sizable enough segment of the Denver community that would do business with a bank called The Women's Bank. The study also demonstrated that it could succeed and be a viable financial institution. That is exactly what happened. It opened on July 14, 1978, with $1 million in first-day deposits. Deposits continued to grow so that at the year's end the bank had 5,000 customers and $13 million in deposits. It was one of the fastest growing new banks in Colorado in 1978 and 1979. The bank was operating 100 percent in the black in just over 10 months.

Why did it succeed? The market need was there. Women, in sufficient numbers, perceived that they were being served inadequately by existing financial institutions. They were willing to move their banking business to a more responsive financial institution.

Global Marketplace

There is one other dimension in competition to be discussed—the global economy. Although it may not directly affect franchises or other small businesses, it can do so indirectly, and franchisees should be aware of its growing importance.

Because of the globalization of the world economy in the 1990s, it is essential to do your marketing analysis in the broadest terms of competition. Look at those products or services that do the job as reasonably and as effectively as you do, or suggest that they can. Once American car franchisees had a lock on their local market. Now, they as well as competitors have bought foreign car franchises to market alongside American brands.

Most businesses affected by foreign competition are now located along the East and West Coasts. In the future, businesses throughout the U.S. will find that they will be increasingly affected by international trade and political decisions.

The following industries have long been a part of international trade: technology, machinery, chemicals, food, stone, clay, glass, rubber, and plastics. If these industries relate in any way to your franchise, you should be alert to any international developments that affect the production, distribution, cost, innovation, shipping, finishing, shortage, or embargo of these items.

Also, be aware of beneficial developments that could enhance your product line, provide more sources of raw and/or finished product, or decrease shipping costs. Also be aware of potential problems. An example of this was the increased difficulty in getting bauxite, an element in aluminum, as political relationships cooled with Jamaica in the 1970s. A similar situation occurred with low-cost manufactured products when the U.S. government threatened to withdraw the most favored nation trading status from China in the early 1990s. There was strong sentiment to do this because of the massacre against student protesters in Beijing. Americans watched the events unfold in their living rooms on television and were outraged. Many a franchisor that was marketing Chinese-made items had to worry about the source of low-cost products for their businesses to sell. If any product or raw materials are important to your franchised business, you need to be aware of changes in their market or trade conditions.

Some businesses today already are affected in international trade and political decisions. Indicators are that more businesses in the future will be affected by those factors. We suggest you evaluate the impact the world market can have on any phase of your business, and then take appropriate action to protect yourself.

Benefits of Competition

Some businesses benefit from competition. In many cases, competition appears to effectively expand the marketplace. For example, in shopping centers, sections often are devoted to similar businesses—shoe stores, book stores, stationery stores, sportswear boutiques, youth-oriented stores, and so forth. It has been shown that customers often will go out of their way to seek out areas where there is competitive selection of particular products. The result is that everyone gets a greater share of the business. In this case, a clustering of similar shops has become beneficial.

This idea has been carried even further, to the concept of shopping centers that cater to a similar segment of the marketplace, such as to upper-middle-class buyers. One-stop shopping is becoming very popular. For instance, a family frequently drives to a shopping center where a variety of similar shops can serve its needs. Because they find a number of stores with similar goods, they are more likely to succeed in their buying efforts.

For example, many shopping centers are designed for convenience and value and are aimed at women shoppers who want to do
all their shopping at once. Today, more than 50 percent of women
are employed. Time has become a very important consideration.
These factors make the placement of one's business near one's competitors a potential benefit to be seriously considered in the future.

It's all too clear that there are many factors to be evaluated when
considering competition. Don't let the variety of issues intimidate
you and your fellow franchisees. This is a task to be undertaken by
franchisee and franchisor in a cooperative manner. It also can be
carried out over a prolonged period of time. A franchisee advisory
council would be an excellent place for this kind of study to be
initiated. Don't back off if you do not have the resources for a full
study. Break off a piece of the puzzle and get started. It might initially be a comparison of competitive advertising. Whatever it is, get
started. Each piece of the puzzle is essential. Each bit of information
contributes to your overall success.

ENDNOTES

[1] Michael E. Porter, *Competitive Strategy*, The Free Press, New
York, NY, 1980.

[2] Ibid.

[3] *The 1992 Franchise Annual*, by Info Press, Lewiston, NY, 1992.

CHAPTER 5

Changes in Market Conditions

Economics—the study of money matters—is not a remote science. It is an all-encompassing and vital part of the atmosphere in which a small business must operate. Understanding the economic impact on our business lives will help us to compete more effectively.

Finance reflects the economic impact on your business. More specifically, it is the management of money, banking, investments, and credit. You may not realize it, but you are always making economic decisions. Allocation of your limited resource—money—accounts for most of your major economic decisions. What is the real cost of an advertisement? From whom do you order supplies? Do you send someone out on company time to buy needed supplies, or is it cheaper to pay higher prices or a surcharge for deliveries? Do you buy or lease company cars or equipment? Do you locate in one part of the city or in the suburbs?

Tax rates, government spending, the supply of money, the availability of credit, and the rate of interest all precipitate economic decision making on your part. Mix in a little local competition, consumer demand for your products and services, a big dose of advertising, and a little (or a lot) of influence from the labor unions, and you have the recipe for either success or failure, depending on the ongoing economic decisions you make.

British economist Alfred Marshall defined economics as the "study of mankind in the ordinary business of life." Textbooks divide the study of economics into essentially two parts: macroeconomics, which focuses on the economy as a whole; and microeconomics, which portrays that part of the economy that is concerned with the behavior of people and organizations in particular markets. Microeconomics focuses on the scarcity of goods and how one makes choices.

To make the very best decisions we can, we have to understand the economy and how it keeps changing. The economy affects most areas of our lives, making economics a social science, an examination of how and why resources are allocated among those who want them. To have the resources we want, we either have to own them or be able to buy or borrow them in the marketplace.

Macroeconomics

In the study of macroeconomics, we look at the system as a whole.[1] Here we're talking about the big picture; water, electricity, transportation, and resources. Most of us in franchising, as individual businesspeople, would have little impact on changing the macro picture. However, there is a way to make your voice heard. That is through trade associations. You can join your local Chamber of Commerce, Association of Manufacturers, retail trade associations, and other like organizations that lobby for and influence change. You can participate in specific activities.

In 1986 I ran and won a local election to be a delegate to the White House Conference on Small Business. I chaired the Colorado delegation's committee on Product Liability and Tort Reform and was a member of the national committee on the same subject. The concern over tort reform and product liability caused these two issues to be joined and to become the number one priority issue for small business. Tort is considered to be a state issue. Many states, including Colorado, have already enacted new legislation on tort reform. Product liability is considered to be a federal issue, as it requires uniformity in manufacturing regulation. A national product liability law appears to be emerging from Congress.

By becoming active in such an organization, you can make your voice heard on important local and national business issues that impact the economic growth, development, and ultimately the survival of your business. I have also served on the board of directors of the State Chamber of Commerce, the Colorado Association of Commerce and Industry, and the Denver Chamber of Commerce, as well as the Colorado Small Business Council. During my tenure we supported issues such as regulatory reform, the development of a new regional airport, the development of a central business district retail mall, and the growth of the regional transportation system. All of the above have or are in the process of coming to fruition. These are specific examples of macro issues that can be influenced by your involvement. These issues can and do impact your business. You may want to expand your franchise to include a stall at a new regional airport or on a central business district mall. You can influence the outcome and thereby affect the future of your business and your community. You'll want to know where the future transportation hubs will be. You can make important things happen. You can be a voice in the macro picture of your business community.

In a speech that Rena Bartos, author, consultant, and former Senior Vice President and Director of Communications Development for J. Walter Thompson, gave to the Committee of 200 at the University of Chicago Graduate School of Business, she outlined five trends that will redefine marketing and advertising.[2] These trends are:

1. The Changing Economy

    a. An increasing amount of income concentrated among the upper one-third of households

    b. A shrinking middle class

    c. A disadvantaged underclass

2. The Changing Role of Women

    a. More than 55 percent of women are in the workforce. The remainder includes those of school age and the elderly. This is a predictor of increased future participation in the workforce.

3. Changing Life Cycle Patterns

a. Only 58 percent of Americans are married.

b. There are almost twice as many two-paycheck marriages as couples who live in the traditional pattern of breadwinner and homemaker-wife.

c. One in four two-paycheck households are over 40 years of age. That will escalate with the aging of baby boomers.

d. Only 33 percent of adults have children under 18 years of age living at home.

4. The Changing Age Composition of America

a. The oldest baby boomers—those born between 1946 and 1964—are already in their mid-40s, and will change the demographics of the nation.

5. Changing Social Values

a. As women are becoming doctors, lawyers, business owners, mayors, judges, and so forth, the image of traditional authority figures changes in our society.

What does all of this mean? It means that by understanding these macro trends and their possible implications for your business, you can help position your franchise for growth in the 1990s and beyond.

Microeconomics

As I indicated earlier, microeconomics is the study of scarcity and of choosing.[3] It deals with the specific allocation of scarce resources. People as individuals and acting on behalf of their businesses make choices. Any business, including franchises, whether large or small, operates within the constraints of a market. Only a handful of companies have a market all to themselves (utilities are a prime example). These businesses are known as monopolies. Microeconomics deals with supply and demand. Supply and demand is the most fundamental market concept that your business operates under, so let's review how it works.

In a market economy, a business produces a supply of products and services that are in demand by others. This differs from the central planning of a communist or socialist regime where planners determine what and how much will be produced and how these items will be distributed. In a market economy, in theory, the more valuable one's work, the more income that should be derived from that work.

Demand is the "propensity to buy."[4] It does not mean the actual purchasing of the item. The propensity is measured relative to other variables. Your propensity to buy most likely will vary with the price. If you are a LePeep's franchisee and serve a $1.99 sit-down breakfast, you could siphon off McDonald's customers who might be taking an Egg McMuffin on the run. Therefore, in addition to price, through the dimension of added perceived value, you have changed the way the customer evaluates the merchandise.

There are other ways to add value. When running Weight Watchers in the Rocky Mountain Region, I addressed the slow summer season with a "Two Week Vacation" value-added package. I allowed members to buy 10 weeks of membership for the price of eight. That definitely increased demand. The key element of supply and demand is competitive pricing and the effective communication of any change in pricing and/or value to your customer base.

Competitive Pricing

As a franchise owner, you must in some way determine the demand for your product, and analyze this demand in light of potential price changes. Generally, the higher the price of your goods or services, the less demand there will be for it. Your franchise may have some control over those prices—that is, may determine that a higher or lower price is justified under certain circumstances. Then again, you might not have a choice but to charge a price that's dictated by the marketplace (e.g., a uniform product such as coal, corn, or concrete, all of which are supplied by many companies and therefore the prices are set by the market, not by an individual firm). Franchisors cannot dictate the end price of a product in the U.S. They can suggest a price, but the ultimate pricing decision is up to you.

Rent and labor costs in Alaska and New York City are considerably higher than U.S. averages. That would be reflected in your prices if you had a franchise there. But keep in mind that arbitrary and unsubstantiated price increases can meet with market resistance. This was found by some discount hair salon franchises in 1989. Independent SuperCuts franchises that raised prices encountered price resistance by customers at certain levels. Most opted to roll back prices to optimum levels. Optimum levels reflect a combination of gross sales, customer retention, and optimum utilization of personnel. Basically, when your franchisor does solid pricing research, it is wise to rely on it.

Franchisees do have initiative power in a market. You can be proactive. For example, Don Wollan, a San Diego-based Burger King franchisee, succeeds in his highly competitive market by monitoring competitors' prices continuously. He shops his competitors and stays aware of any special value pricing that they may have added to their product line.

If your business can create some "special difference" in its product, even if that difference is only the result of marketing, the price charged can differ somewhat from your competitors. By just how much is determined by what is called "elasticity of demand." That is, given a substantial price difference, your customer may decide to move to a competitor. However, if that difference is only a few cents and the "service with a smile" or whatever the preferred service is turns out to be worth it to the customer, he just may pay the higher price and remain your loyal customer.

The measurement of the elasticity of demand is important to understand. If you lower your prices, you know that sales will increase; that is, the demand will increase. Elasticity of demand measures the amount of change.[5] It answers the question, how many more customers will I get when the price is reduced? How much do I have to lower prices in order to improve revenue and/or increase profits? If, for instance, a 10 percent price change impacted demand by 25 percent, that item would be considered relatively elastic. If that same 10 percent price change caused only a 5 percent change in demand, the item would be considered to be relatively inelastic. The many franchised gasoline dealers understand this. Price changes sometime precipitate price wars to offset loss of clientele. You probably have a favorite gas station. A few cents differential might not cause you to drive out of the way for a refill. But, a big enough differential will likely cause you to seek the saving. At that price—maybe it would be 5 cents a gallon, or 10 cents a gallon, wherever the market makes the determination there is a significant change in demand—there is considered to be a large elasticity of demand.

Don Wollan, the Burger King franchisee, has developed a competitive stance with pricing. He maintains special value pricing for a hamburger at 39 cents. This remains his lead item. His french fries and drinks are just slightly higher than the competition. They are not high enough to drive the consumer away. However, when he has items on his menu that cannot be purchased elsewhere—the Burger King Whopper for instance—he can price that at a premium. Because he has researched his competitors, and because he has used pricing as a marketing tool, he has been successful in significantly improving volume as well as profitability in his four Burger King franchises.

Another example of competitive or differential pricing is the convenience store franchise. Many of these operations are nationwide or regionally based franchises. They are known to advertise "time savings" as opposed to "cost savings." In this busy world with more demands on our time, many consumers may very well find time to be a more limited resource than money. The convenience store market, recognizing this, has moved into this service niche, where prices may be higher, but service is faster than in a supermarket.

Monitoring Business Cycles

Each franchised business operates in the context of the whole industry or market in the total economy. A drop in the overall business activity, typically called a recession, may very well signify a drop in the demand for products or services. A franchised businessperson may find that, because of steadily rising unemployment caused by tight money and higher interest rates, customers aren't spending as freely as they used to. Here are some examples of how national and local changes might affect franchisees:

Let's say that in its attempt to slow the general rise in prices, the Federal Reserve Board of Governors increases its discount (interest) rate. Now you, as a franchisee, walk into the bank and ask your banker for a loan. The loan officer quotes you a higher interest rate than you were expecting. You say "Thanks, but no thanks . . ." and decide to make do without the loan. This happens with your fellow businesses, too, and loan demand drops off. As you and other franchisees hold back on expansion plans, or slow up your businesses because you didn't get a loan, your employees are the next ones affected. Production levels off, and then begins to fall, and higher rates of unemployment result. Some workers may be eligible for unemployment compensation, but it doesn't usually stretch as far as their paychecks did. As households adjust to their lower incomes, only necessities are included in the new budget. One possible result of the Federal Reserve Board's decision to slow up the economy, utilizing monetary policy, could be a reduction in the sale of your goods and services. Some businesses would be more sensitive to monetary policy than others. This would be more likely in the case where the product or service is highly discretionary, or if the price of the product is high.

In another plausible situation, you may own a fast-food franchise. Most households allocate just so much money toward eating out. In a recession, that allocation may be reduced. For you to hold on to your customers and maintain your market share, you may have to do more marketing—increase value pricing and do more value-added promotions. These promotions may cut into your overall profitability and have an impact on a whole array of other business decisions.

Business cycles aren't always a result of deliberate actions by fiscal and monetary authorities, but their everyday decisions can and do affect our economic lives. In the late 1980s and early 1990s monetary policy has been a management tool used by the Federal Reserve Board to attempt to fine-tune the economy. We have to know about those decisions, and about other aspects of the economy as a whole, and become alert to the changes that are going to affect our sales, costs, and profits.

Once your market analysis indicates that there are customers willing to buy your product or service—that is, that there is effective demand for it—you then face cost decisions in creating an inventory. All your resources (labor, materials, sales outlets, utilities, equipment) must be analyzed so that all costs can be met (including the cost of management and entrepreneurship, or risk-taking).

We have just emerged from a very long period of prosperity and market growth. Now, we find the country in a recession. These varying periods of market growth and retraction are called the business cycle. They are a natural part of a market economy. Sometimes they're referred to as "boom" and "bust" cycles, although they are usually not that dramatic. In a "boom" or expanding economy, consumer spending increases and causes increased investment in goods and services. Plant and inventory investment is a result. When this phase is maximized, when too many plants are producing too many goods and too much distribution is taking place, the cycle reverses.[6] Too much inventory causes a slowdown in orders, backed up inventory, discounted pricing, smaller corporate margins, and labor layoffs.

There is often a psychological component. Because of the impact of media and the proliferation of information, the news travels fast. We hear this negative news and decide that it's not the right time to buy that furniture, additional clothing, and definitely not the right time for impulse shopping. In other words, the market economy self-corrects.

Although the national economy establishes the climate within which a franchised business and its owner must operate, franchisees are primarily concerned about the local climate that their businesses have to operate in. It's this "particular market"—the one you have to face each day when you turn the key in the door—that we'll look at next. However, still keep in mind the effect of government spending, taxation, and monetary policies on business cycles and ultimately your business.

Record Keeping

At one time in our history, an individual with a new idea could simply produce and sell goods out of her home or small shop; costs were easily determined, net profit was easily calculated, and profits were deducted from revenues.

Today, in our modern economy, even the smallest, one-person business must keep records and spend some time on financial planning. As the business grows, even more information is required by government agencies enforcing the Consumer Product Safety Act, the Occupational Safety and Health Act, the Environmental Protection Act, and a host of other regulatory laws passed in the past 20 to 30 years. Add to these the local regulations, and each franchisee has a challenge. This is the point where your franchisor should step in and provide you with record-keeping systems that reflect your needs to help keep you up to speed with your specific industry. If your franchisor will not step in, it often would be to your advantage to develop an appropriate record-keeping system in your franchise advisory council.

There are numerous computer software programs geared specifically toward the record-keeping requirements of small businesses. For example, Windows-based programs are user-friendly in all applications. People with minimal computer skills can readily benefit from these programs.

Once again, if usable software is not readily available and if your franchisor will not produce the required software, it could be beneficial for a group of franchisees to band together to share the costs and the work involved in developing the needed software.

One extremely important form of record-keeping to have in place is a cash flow analysis. You may be overwhelmed with orders, and keep buying inventory, forgetting short-term obligations. Rent must be paid; as must utilities, phones, insurance, and wages. You need to know when these bills are coming in and when they'll have to be paid. When you have good cash flow records, you can address specific needs with lines of credit, terms, and the establishment of priorities.

Charlotte Taylor, author of *Women and the Business Game* said it best when she said, "the key to having a good tracking system of your company's health is to develop it early, keep it simple, and keep it up to date."[7] Whether your records are kept on a computer or done by hand, initiate a system early. Make sure it's a system you're comfortable with. If you cannot figure out how to set up the system efficiently and effectively, get help. Your franchisor should be on the front line in developing such systems. It is a primary service that should be provided to franchisees.

If you've been unsuccessful in getting your franchisor to take on this responsibility, definitely initiate a team effort among franchisees. Share responsibilities and costs. Then, discuss your industry's specific requirements with an accountant or financial adviser. Get a good system in place. If you set up a uniform set of accounts, all franchisees can share data, develop industry norms, evaluate variables, and individually and as a group benefit from the ability to research results.

Your system should include the following:[8]

1. Cash receipts

2. Cash disbursements

3. Sales

4. Purchases

5. Payroll date

6. Equipment (the firm's assets)

7. Inventory

8. Accounts receivable (what the customers owe the firm)

9. Accounts payable (what the firm owes its creditors and suppliers)

In addition to cash flow statements, you'll require this information to produce a balance sheet. The balance sheet reflects the net worth of your company. It includes company's assets and liabilities, reflected as short and long term, as well as shareholder's equity. The shareholder's equity is the result after total liabilities are deducted from total assets. This is an important way to measure the value of your business. Most small businesses have their accounting firm produce their balance sheet. However, if you have filled out an application for a personal loan, you already have filled out a personal net worth statement or a personal balance sheet. If you're comfortable with the concept, you could readily do this for your business.

Another important record is your income statement, which has three characteristics:

1. It is a measure of income less expenses.

2. It measures results over a period of time.

3. It is an estimate.

This statement is also popularly referred to as a Profit and Loss Statement. Whatever, it is a very important report card on the health of your business. With today's computer reporting technology, there is no reason your business cannot have such a statement readily available for review.

Competing in the Tightening Labor Market

The 1990s will present a special problem to franchisees. Some are already experiencing the problem of a significantly tightening labor market. We have experienced the end of the so-called "baby boomer" population explosion that followed World War II. The oldest of the baby boomers will soon be turning 50. The young people who worked the counters and ovens of McDonald's and Burger King are in ever shorter supply. (Signs have been seen in New England eateries advertising for staff at $6.75 an hour. This is while our Congress and President fight over whether our minimum wage should be $4.25 or $4.55 an hour.) Some franchisors are addressing this problem creatively. Arby's has introduced computerized ordering devices. The customer steps to the counter, and places his or her order by computer. This reduces the pressure on staff.

Increasingly, such innovations will be introduced by innovative franchisors providing their franchisees with a competitive edge. As a franchisee, it is to your advantage to put pressure on your franchisor, persuading him to innovate and to take full advantage of today's technology as a way of reducing staff demands.

The demographics of the work force will impact your business too. Besides too few workers, we have too many under-trained and unskilled workers in the U.S. labor force. According to Dr. Lester C. Thorow, Dean of the Sloane School of Business at the Massachusetts Institute of Technology, we will eventually have a two-tier work force in the U.S.—those that are college and university trained, and a class of unskilled workers. Because of this predicted labor shortage, it is going to fall on the shoulders of businesses to train these workers.[9] SuperCuts, the major hair care franchise, has implemented extensive training of hairstylists in order to meet their standards and to offset a short labor supply. They have initiated this action instead of just trusting the marketplace to fill the demand. It's highly unlikely that you as an individual franchisee can implement change. However, in cooperation with your franchisor and fellow franchisees, like SuperCuts, you can bring about specific and beneficial changes.

Staying Competitive

For most franchisees who are providing a product or a service, your single most important consideration is staying competitive. Competition influences our business decisions to some extent. Competition means that some substitutes for your product exist. The easier the customer can substitute another product for yours, the greater your competition will be.

The quantity demanded of your product is subject to both internal and external forces. You usually can control the internal factors, such as the prices you charge for your products and services and the cost of doing business. This book is designed to help you do just that. Nevertheless, you'll usually have to deal with external conditions as well.

As the economy changes, as businesses grow larger or smaller, as industries are born or die, as new products are introduced and technologies improved, and as society's values change, all ultimately have an effect on the marketplace. They'll affect what products or services are needed and wanted. Take for example, National Video franchise. Thousands of people invested in small video rental shops throughout the country and initially prospered. Then competition developed in every supermarket and in supermarket-type video rental outfits like Blockbuster.

Blockbuster is also a franchise, but better geared to corporate investment, as opposed to the mom & pop type operators of the National Video stores. Blockbuster provides a much larger selection of videos, more copies of every title, automated procedures to identify clientele, as well as a well-established and highly professional marketing program. In scenarios such as this, the competitive marketplace had changed dramatically, leaving many franchisees in a lurch.

During the 20th century, the American economy has evolved from domination by small business to a highly integrated and sophisticated national and international economy, with very large companies providing many jobs, goods, and services, and holding the largest assets. But even with the American economy dominated by industrial giants, change is clearly under way. Franchised business is flourishing. Small business is here to stay, and is making an impact on our economy. There are more than six million small businesses providing goods and services, government revenues, and profits. Of these, almost 600,000 are franchises.[10] These franchises, as you well know, operate side by side with big businesses. Sometimes they compete with them, more often supplying them with products or services.

Franchisees also have the value-added benefit of professional advertising and marketing, access to product and training, research and development enhanced by good management, financial planning, and record-keeping, all supported by successful franchisors. Their future appears bright.

ENDNOTES

[1] Albert V. Bowed, *Economics*, South-Western Publishing Company, Cincinnati, OH, 1974.

[2] Rena Bartos, from a seminar on Business Creation and Development Strategies, University of Chicago Graduate School, November 5, 1987.

[3] Albert V. Bowed, *Economics*, South-Western Publishing Co., Cincinnati, OH, 1974.

[4] Ibid.

[5] Ibid.

[6] Ibid.

[7] Charlotte Taylor, *Women and the Business Game*, Venture Concepts Press, Washington, D.C., 1980.

[8] Ibid.

[9] Dr. Lester C. Thurow, *Head To Head*, Morrow, 1992.

[10] "The Future of Franchising, A Study for the International Franchise Association," The Anisette Group, Washington, DC, December 1985.

CHAPTER 6

Setting Marketing Goals

All businesspersons, whether they are just starting out or already up and running, need to define well-thought-out goals for their businesses. These goals should be written down so they can be periodically reviewed. In evaluating goals, sometimes we have to trade off one goal against another. Sometimes we have to work to achieve one goal at a particular time in order to lay down the basis for achieving another goal. However, there are some universal goals for businesses. We're going to review these from a franchisee's perspective.

Profitability

A very logical first goal could be profitability. Profitability is essential if your business is going to succeed. Profitability—unless you are seeking out a nonprofit corporation, a charity, or a similar type of welfare organization—must be an essential element in the planning for the success of your business organization. If it is not at the top of

your list of goals, you might be more comfortable and more successful working for someone other than for yourself. Having a strongly
ingrained profit motive is essential to being in business for yourself.
Profit levels of most firms make up a relatively small percentage of
the firm's total sales. In the case of franchises, it is especially important that good profit levels be maintained, as profits are shared
between franchisee and franchisor.

The goal of profitability does not preclude idealistic goals toward
social and economic change. When Nancy Fairchild, a Colorado
resident, left U.S. West Corporation, she came to my firm to help
her buy a franchise. At first she was interested in a health type
bakery. When we had discussed her life-style motivators, it became
clear that she didn't like tight schedules and inflexible routines. We
came to the conclusion that no business could be more scheduled
and less flexible than a bakery.

We decided to focus on the health and/or ecological aspect of the
business, and to look for a franchise that allowed more flexibility in
scheduling. She eventually opted to become the franchisee for Foliage Design Systems, a franchisor that provides interiorscaping. That
is, they market and promote beautiful interiors utilizing creative
plantings. These plants are leased and tended with nontoxic chemicals. In fact, a major sales program is the curing of sick building
syndrome through the abundant use of natural plants in interior
decorating schemes. Foliage Design clientele includes hotel, restaurants, office buildings, offices, retail stores, and some residential clients.

There are many other franchises that have a health or ecological
benefit. You can include health-oriented restaurants, health food
stores, and exercise franchises. You can maintain both the idealistic
and the profit motive in your franchise, along with personal goals.
I'd also like to say that you may be idealistic in other ways. Once
you are an established franchise in your community, you can participate in fund-raising activities for charities and generally work on
behalf of the community in organizations like Rotary and Lions. The
Rotary Club, of which I am a member, has helped a local homeless
shelter, a locally based Japanese University, and a program giving
immunizations to children from poorer families. Most of the members of Rotary are professionals and self-employed men and women.
There are many other worthwhile community-based organizations
that you and your business can help. While running Weight Watch-

ers, we sponsored a team in the March of Dimes annual Team Walk-A-Thon. In addition, we gave out oranges to hungry and thirsty walkers. To be sure that we were good, environmentally concerned citizens, we provided extra baskets for the orange peels. It's fun to be community spirited, and it does win "brownie points" and sometimes recognition for you and your business.

Domination and Segmentation of the Market

One goal as a franchise owner might be to dominate your market, whether defined in terms of geographical area, product, or price. Another goal could be to dominate a certain segment of the marketplace. The theory of marketing segmentation, or niche marketing, says that, if there is a segment of the marketplace that is unserved or perceives itself as unserved, you can successfully develop a business around a product or service for that market.

We see marketing segmentation at every stage of our lives. In the auto field, a Volkswagen or a Cadillac both can take us to the same place in roughly the same amount of time. However, each have completely different product images—the comfort level, the decor, the status appeal. Those images are mainly a result of marketing and advertising, and not of firsthand product knowledge. One car is billed as a practical vehicle; the other represents status and success and appeals to those wishing to project a certain image.

Cosmetics provide another example. Whether women buy Charlie cologne, Charles of the Ritz, or Maybelline, they are buying relatively similar products. Charlie has the appeal of youth, Charles of the Ritz, of status and exclusivity; and Maybelline, of convenience and economy.

We also see marketing segmentation in many businesses: in an Hispanic bookstore, a neighborhood newspaper, a dress shop for large women, a sports magazine, a disco or classical record shop, an exclusive men's shop, a secondhand store. In each case, the owner has determined that his business would serve a particular segment of the general marketplace, and has developed a vehicle to reach that segment. Of course, franchisors also have moved into segmented markets. Examples of franchises aimed at particular market segments include discount haircut salons, quick lube change operations, drive-through fast-food operations, and home-delivered pizza and Chinese foods. Still others provide mobile-based glass repair, limousine services, and one-hour photography. The list goes on and on.

The Age of Specialization

Specialization also has taken hold in many professions, and though it seems different at first glance, it is really the same as marketing segmentation. We certainly are aware that there are specialists among physicians (internists, pediatricians, gynecologists). Among dentists there are endontists, pediodontists, and orthodontists. Among lawyers, there are traditional law firms and the new legal clinics, specializing in lower-cost, more routine services. Other lawyers specialize in family law, criminal law, bankruptcy, banking, and real estate law.

Even insurance companies have defined their marketing segment and such specialized insurance companies as American Banker's Insurance (which has developed specific products and services for the banking industry) have achieved a high level of success. One example of insurance segmentation of the marketplace is the decision described by Bernard Weiss, manager of life, health, and financial services of Travelers Corporation of Hartford, Connecticut, to target women as a growth market, a decision based on industry research.

How can you segment your market? There are a number of potential segments on the basis of sex, age, income level, education level, occupation, ethnic background, homeowners versus renters, geographic location, merchandise services available, and probably a dozen other ways.

Franchisees have a special advantage in market segmentation. Simply put, you can be more flexible, continue to keep your finger on the pulse of changes in consumer interest and demand. You can then anticipate trends, make changes, and remain successful within your chosen field. You can readily see what inflexibility did to a company like Chrysler in the late 1970s and early 1980s, when the public demand for Chrysler's large cars took a 180-degree turn, leaving its product line less competitive. The company was on the brink of bankruptcy and had to turn to the federal government to bail them out of trouble.

Franchises, under the leadership of strong and innovative franchisors, can be more flexible and responsive to the market. McDonald's flexibility was demonstrated by its introduction of the Egg

McMuffin, thereby starting fast-food breakfast service. Weight Watchers revamped its food plan successfully. Reacting to the grand move of women into the workplace in the 1970s, Weight Watchers added more pre-prepared, packaged, and ready-to-eat products to its eating plan, and it has continued to innovate and to introduce more changes annually. (More recently, though, the changes have appeared to the author to be more cosmetic than substantive.) Most Pak Mail franchisees have added the making of keys to their service roster.

There is really no limit on the ways that your market can be segmented. You are limited only by marketing dollars and by the variety of products and services. But first you or your franchisor must determine your marketing goal so that you can be assured you're focusing on the most productive market segment. Until you determine who it is you want to reach, you can't determine where you are going to locate your business, how much space you'll require, how you are going to decorate, and what kind of equipment you are going to need.

Marketing Plan

Before embarking on an advertising or public relations program, you should look at the bigger marketing picture. Marketing encompasses the many activities involved in the moving of goods and services from producers to consumers. This includes selling, advertising, packaging, public relations, promotions, and merchandising. Since you have limited money, you must allocate the amount you will spend, then develop a plan for spending that allocation. The following are the steps in developing a marketing plan for your franchise[1]:

1. Write a mission statement. An example of a statement can be the following, which is based on the mission statement of a national franchisor: "This franchisor wants to provide marketing leadership to the system through the development of innovative and effective marketing programs to increase national sales and to build its franchise image into a national brand."

2. Research your target market.

3. Know your competition.

4. Determine your position or segment in the larger marketplace. Will you be the largest, fastest-growing, the highest-quality operation?

5. Establish marketing goals and objectives. For example, what percentage of gross sales will be required to be reinvested into local and national marketing programs?

6. Price and package to establish your objectives.

7. Find the expert help you need to succeed.

8. Develop your marketing budget.

9. Plan on success.

With your plan in hand you'll be ready to go forward. This plan could be developed under the auspices of the franchisor or a franchise advisory council. It can definitely and very effectively be a regional franchisee project. Don't let this plan-making intimidate you. You will be better for having gone through this self-examination.

Market Research

When it comes to packaging your service or product you must ask how and to whom will it be marketed: Where will you advertise? What newspapers will best reach your audience? Will you use radio or television? One of the beauties of franchising is that the answers to these questions should come from your franchisor. A franchisor that is doing its job should be conducting market research to answer these questions. Weight Watchers had determined that women were its market. Although men were welcome to participate, little or no advertising dollars were allocated to attract them. All advertisements were geared to women's success stories. All advertising was geared to shows that had predominantly female audiences. In contrast, Super-Cuts determined through research that their market was predominantly male. Women were welcome to SuperCuts, but their marketing always featured men. Again, determining your market position gives you the ability to exploit it efficiently and effectively.

An important step in establishing these goals is to be well-informed about the people you expect to buy your product or service. For this, you need marketing research.The first step is to try to work through your franchisor. It is very appropriate for a franchisor to spearhead efforts to determine the organizational goals. If this help isn't forthcoming, working through a franchisee association is in order. The franchisee council can initiate such a project and solicit the assistance of the franchisor. When it comes to matters that only affect your particular franchise operation, you can do your own survey, use students, or hire professionals. It can be limited or on a large scale. You might be able to interest a local Chamber of Commerce in underwriting such a survey or study if it could be generally beneficial to the business or to the general community. Whatever approach you use, you will likely find that the study will pay for itself in that you'll make fewer errors and be better able to move more quickly using the sound information you've gathered.

Your best friend for accessing marketing data is your central public library. Up-to-date libraries have computerized data files. It's as easy as entering the subject that you're interested in onto the computer. The computer then brings up information on books, magazines, and articles that pertain to your subject of interest.

Marketing and demographic data is also available from the Bureau of the Census; the Small Business Administration; Housing and Urban Development (HUD); Urban Renewal Authorities; Chambers of Commerce; city, county, and state planning and development offices; and other public and private business and community development-type agencies. This data can save you hours in your own marketing efforts, and can help you in your long-range planning efforts. It's also free. You already have paid for it with your taxes. Now it's up to you to take advantage of it.

Another source of management help to small businesspeople is SCORE (Service Core of Retired Executives). These are retired executives who lend their business expertise to small businesses. You can reach them through your local Small Business Administration office.

Advertising

The prerequisite for successful advertising is knowing who you are serving and who you want to reach, and then finding the best, most economical way to reach that market. If you're in a small community and have one radio and one newspaper outlet, the question is academic. For the vast majority of small businesses, though, there are overwhelming numbers of alternatives available to you. It will take some effort on your part to understand them, and then to determine which one is the best for your business. Spending your advertising dollars efficiently is essential to an effective and successful marketing plan. What if you're not sure who makes up your best market? How can you determine this? What if your financial and personnel resources are so limited that you can't do the necessary marketing research? One possible solution would be to contact the marketing department of a local college or university. They recruit marketing students to do studies for local businesses. The benefit to the students is that they are working on real-life business problems; the benefit to the businessperson is that the project can be accomplished at minimal cost. The projects are supervised by qualified marketing professors. Usually the business is asked to pick up only the real costs incurred by the students.

Advice from an Expert

One woman who is an expert in advertising is Lois Geraci Ernst, the Chief Executive Officer (CEO) of ATW, a New York-based advertising and marketing firm. ATW stands for Advertising To Women, Inc. Ms. Ernst fully understands the power of segmenting the market, and then delivering to that market. She has been the prime mover of many of the top 10 brands of perfume marketed in the U.S., as well as such products as Silkience hair care, which created $150 million in new business in the first year of its launch. Her creative, conceptual product work on the Easy Spirit shoe resulted in the development of a $300 million division at U.S. Shoe focused on this product line. (Remember the Easy Spirit pumps playing basketball to the message "Looks like a pump, feels like a sneaker"?)

Lois Geraci Ernst has some important words regarding marketing for those of you who may be depending on your franchisor to handle your advertising and marketing. Her point is that, regardless of this help, creativity based on local marketing conditions is usually beneficial. She has set forth four basic rules. They are the best, basic set of recommendations I have ever seen for effective marketing.

1. *Know your customer.* Who buys your product? This is essential to spending your limited advertising dollars effectively.

2. *Make people feel something.* What does your product or service communicate to your customer? Emotion is the key. Not just

the facts. They must also feel something. Are you selling confidence, security, love, freedom, excitement?

3. *Tell the truth.* If you don't, it will come back to haunt you.

4. *Don't be dull.* There are too many people competing for your customers' dollars. Make sure that your message grabs them. You have to control what your product or service communicates to your customer.

Most franchisees are responsible for spending their own advertising dollars, either for their unit franchise or as part of a franchise advertising cooperative. The latter is frequently set up by the franchisor. The following information is important if you are responsible for the placement of your advertising.

Which Media for You?

Once you have determined a market segment, how do you reach it? Your first thought will likely be your local newspaper. Will it be the large city edition? If so, which part of the paper? Will it be with hard news, business news, sports, entertainment, society, fashion? You'll have to check the newspaper for its demographic profiles of these sections. In print media, you'll want to be able to set up an advertisement. You'll need to know the width of a column inch, the height of the paper in inches, and the price per column inch. You'll want to know if a contract is offered. There are significant price differentials in print advertising based on the size of an advertising contract. When you are in a group of franchisees with pooled resources, your advertising dollars will go a long way. The message of the ad need only be run first; individual units and addresses and/or phone numbers accompany the ad. You not only need fewer ads, you pay less. Regarding production, you'll need to know if it's black and white or color production.

In the analysis of cost in media, including print media, we are talking about the cost per 1,000 readers or viewers or listeners (CPM). Now we look more seriously at the cost per prospect (CPP). You may get a low CPM, but find that they are not likely targets for your product or service. In the end that can be more costly.[2]

There are also specialized magazines that sell ads. A few come to mind: *Sports Afield, Lears, Working Women, Architectural Digest.* Just in one state, there is the *Rocky Mountain Magazine, Colorado Business, Colorado Lifestyles,* and the *Denver Business Journal.* Most areas of the country have magazines with local appeal.

When choosing these magazines as vehicles for your ads, you must ask: Does this magazine appeal to singles, to youth, to sports fans, to working women, to small business owners, or larger corporations? Does it appeal to your clientele? Does the magazine sales office have information to demonstrate it will reach your customer? If the answer is yes, it may be a very good place to locate your ads. Trade magazines are also good places for certain businesses to place ads. The same questions regarding CPM and CPP, and column width and length as applied in newspaper advertising, apply in magazine advertising.

Radio stations consciously carve out segments of the market that they intend to serve. They may be programmed as 24-hour news stations or classic rock, country, classical, and so forth. They also have specific demographics to tell you the audience for their particular type of programming. Traditionally sports-oriented stations have a high listenership among men. All news formats tend to attract higher-income, better-educated listeners. And disco, pop, and rock stations cater to youth. Radio has perhaps the most highly specialized audiences. Whether your market is teens, homemakers, professionals, the elderly, investors, or minorities, you can target them with radio. Radio is also the most intimate form of media. It walks with people, runs with joggers, keeps driver's company, wakes people up, keeps them entertained, helps them to relax, and allows them to use their imaginations.

In radio, you'll want to know the WATTS of the station, which is its power and what influences its range. You'll also want to know what the ADI is, that is, the area of dominant influence.[3]

What about telemarketing? An automotive service franchisee utilizes telemarketing to develop new business. Telemarketing entails hiring and training an individual or a specialized telemarketing firm to solicit clients for you. Telemarketing, when done properly, can successfully expand your customer base. However, when it it done poorly, you risk antagonizing current and potential customers. Most often, you'll require the services of a professional to establish and execute a program for you, or to teach you how to establish an in-house program successfully.

Television has to be segmented into networks and cable. The networks break out demographics by shows. Different shows attract different viewers. (An exception is the Fox network, which seeks to attract young viewers.) However, cable viewers are attracted to specific stations. CNN is all news and information-oriented. Disney is family-oriented. MTV uses its music format to attract teenagers. Each cable station has a general profile and seeks to maintain its share of that audience. Information regarding the audience can help you reach the right audience at a reasonable price.

In evaluating the purchase of television time, recognize that the price is influenced by the success of the particular program and whether the "time purchase" is prime time or not. The break-out hours for general purchase are usually:[4]

Morning	Monday through Friday	6–9 a.m.
Daytime	Monday through Friday	9 a.m.–3 p.m.
Early fringe	Monday through Friday	3–6 p.m.
Prime Access	Monday through Saturday	6–7 p.m.
Prime Time	Monday through Saturday	7–10 p.m.
	Sunday	6–10 p.m.
Late News	Monday through Sunday	10–10:30 p.m.

Media on the Move

This group includes trade shows, which have proven to be very valuable to companies. I recently attended a home show. The local Decorating Den Franchise Area Director had taken a large, centrally located space and parked a van with home decorating samples. It was far more popular than the standard booth. People could walk right up to the van, see the fabrics, decorating items, and pictures. At any trade show, you can see active franchisee involvement.

Cinema advertising has become more popular. You have a captive audience waiting for the movie to start. Local franchises can tell their story by way of film or slides at various theaters.

Sporting events also have become popular spots for advertising. The local Nutri-System franchisee pays for instant replays at the Denver Broncos home games.

Outdoor, billboard, and bench advertising is blitz-like in that its audience can generally only be segmented on the basis of region or neighborhood.

The choices are as varied as one's imagination. I've even seen advertising in ladies' rest rooms. There undoubtedly will continue to be new ways to reach your market. Keep your marketing plan updated annually. Keep an open mind and share with your fellow franchisees.

Promotion and Public Relations

You may be confused by the difference between advertising, public relations, and promotion. Public relations guru Gloria Zigner, president of Costa Mesa, California-based Gloria Zigner and Associates, describes the difference among the three in a memorable way. When the circus comes to town and you see a sign announcing its arrival, that's advertising. When the sign is hanging off the sides of an elephant marching down Main Street, that's promotion. When the elephant is parading on the mayor's lawn and the press has been called in to cover it, that's public relations. Advertising is essential, because you pay for the message, and have absolute control over the product presented to the public. Promotion is attention getting, and involves a monetary investment to do it correctly. Public relations technically costs nothing, has some element of luck, and you cannot absolutely control the outcome. Still, good public relations has enormous credibility in the eyes of the public, and can be worth its weight in gold.

For example, when running Weight Watchers of the Rocky Mountain Region, I was interviewed for the evening news on a promotion that we had tied in to the March of Dimes campaign. Unfortunately, that day, Elvis Presley died. Needless to say, the death of Elvis was the more newsworthy story, and the more tragic one. The lesson is that publicity is risky. Your story easily can be bumped when something of greater importance occurs. That's just what happened, and my interview was deleted by the station. (They could not have canceled advertising.) The public relations opportunity was lost. However, at other times, participation in Walk-A-Thons, Health Fairs, Telethons, and so forth all have resulted in first-rate publicity for Weight Watchers.

If you are unsure of preparing your own public relations material, there are excellent public relations firms available to guide you through the development and execution of such a program suitable to boost your business in the community.

As an aside, Gloria Zigner says another area of tremendous importance is media training. Should you get the opportunity to be interviewed for radio or television, you should be prepared to present your case in a concise manner. Another reason for this training is that you will be prepared in the event of an emergency at your franchise. Hopefully it will never happen, but you also may be called upon for an interview during a crisis, such as an armed robbery, or—your worst nightmare—contaminated food in your restaurant, defective parts in products, or whatever other type of disaster that would pertain to your business. I would encourage you to ask your franchisor or franchisee advisory council to address the issue of media training and to assist you in being prepared for having to be a spokesperson in these sorts of crises.

Sometimes, POM Will Do the Trick

Nevertheless, sometimes just plain, old-fashioned creativity can shoot you to the top. Church's Chicken franchisee T. Scott Gross has established what he calls P.O.M. This stands for Positively Outrageous Marketing, which includes anything that has the following elements:

1. Random and unexpected

2. Out of proportion to the circumstance

3. Invitation to the customer to play

4. Induces extreme customer loyalty

5. Positive, compelling word of mouth

The basis is fun and entertainment. His franchise contract says that he can't sell gourmet cookies. Nothing in the agreement says he can't give them away. This he does. He also provides drive-thru windshield-wiping service. His name has become synonymous with great service and fun. Without discounting, while embracing P.O.M., Glass's sales have increased 49.8 percent in 1990 and 18.8 percent in

1991. As a franchisee, remember that you have room to innovate in marketing and sales.[5]

Business Consulting Services

Another source of help through universities has been the establishment, by government grant, of a number of Small Business Assistance Centers whose thrust is to help small businesspersons in rural areas. Their goal is to stabilize and expand existing businesses, and aid in the establishment of new enterprises primarily, but not exclusively, in rural areas. If you have not had market research provided to you by your franchisor, and you do not have a franchise advisory council in which to pool your resources to benefit from such research, this could be a solution. This most likely would occur in the case of a newly established franchisor.

Some states have provided publications specifically designed to help small businesspersons get started. One example is Ohio's Starting and Operating a Small Business in Ohio. Another is Doing Business in Colorado, prepared for the Division of Commerce by the Business Research Division, Graduate School of Business Administration, University of Colorado.

Most franchisees cannot afford to assign their marketing and advertising program out to a professional. A considerable amount of money can be saved by taking advantages of the tips in this chapter. Even a small business should avail itself of the marketing and promotional opportunities available in its market. It helps your business. It improves the image and visibility of your franchise. It helps add to your pride as a franchisee.

ENDNOTES

[1] Marketing Director, 1991, CPSI Marketing Services, Englewood, CO.

[2] Ibid.

[3] Ibid.

[4] Ibid.

[5] T. Scott Glass, "Outrageous Service Keeps them Laughing," *Nation's Business*, March 1992, p. 6.

CHAPTER 7

Setting Prices

Establishing a price for your product involves both determining your costs and knowing your competition. In general, prices charged for items must not be out-of-line with the prices of your competitors.

Small differences in price may or may not matter—that's up to your value-conscious buyers. Remember, your franchisor can only recommend prices; they cannot be dictated. It is important to heed your franchisor's advice, though, if it has been based on careful research.

There is a story in a recent issue of *Inc.* magazine about the Vermont grocer who determined his low price was what he paid to his supplier and his high price was the price charged by competition. If it were that simple, we'd have no need to discuss pricing strategies.

In reality, though, each business must set a pricing strategy.[1] The following are some strategies you might consider appropriate to your business:

1. To increase sales.

2. To increase market share.

3. To maximize cash flow or profit.

4. To deter competition from entering your niche.

5. To lower demand so as not to have to raise production capacity.

6. To increase trial, that is to get more people to try your product or service.

Pricing Components

Pricing is a marketing decision, a sales decision, and a financial decision. The complexity of it makes it imperative that you analyze the components of your prices before setting them.[2] For instance, how do your customers or potential customers view your prices?

You can ask them in a test of a new product, or you might ask a number of customers what they think a particular product will cost them.

You may need to review the channels of distribution. Are you the originator of the product or service, or are you the middleman? Do you use a middleman? Your position in the distribution cycle will influence the price you can set.

You also should study the pricing strategies of your competition, and assess the compatibility of your pricing strategy with your company's image. Under most circumstances, you can't set Cadillac prices in a Chevrolet neighborhood.

Tricia Sheriff, a Foliage Design franchisee, was already in the retail florist business when she considered expansion into the commercial market. One of her prime considerations in selecting a franchise, as opposed to starting from scratch, was the help she received in pricing products and services. This is a very competitive industry, according to Tricia, and a mistake can put your business under. Although she wasn't required by law to follow the franchisor's pricing practices, she relied on the knowledge and experience of the franchisor in this confusing area. Some franchisors, like Creative Asset Management, maintain a policy of flexibility in pricing. The franchisor provides a copyrighted investment program, known as "Start Now," to its franchisees. The program is fee-based and helps end users to invest 100 percent of their money in no-load mutual funds and non-commissionable financial products. The company has attracted accountants, tax preparers, casualty insurance agents and others as franchisees. Their objective is to provide financial services without a conflict of interest on the part of the adviser. In this case, depending on the overhead, the clientele, and the role and relationship of the franchisee to the client (i.e., if the franchisee is their accountant), the franchisee is encouraged to set appropriate hourly rates.

If you believe that unique circumstances reflective of your market have not been taken into consideration by your franchisor, this chapter will help you select from among a number of available pricing alternatives.

Cost-Plus or Full Cost Pricing

Several studies show that most companies use some form of "cost-plus" pricing. This is a method that sets prices to cover all direct costs plus some percentage markup. One way is to estimate the average of variable costs of production and marketing, add a charge for overhead, and then add a percentage markup for profits.

For example, say you own a gift store that has a variety of items for sale. Your cost of a particular item is $20. You determine that the average cost of marketing each item in your store is 10 percent. You then add $2 to the cost of that item. You also have determined that overhead is 50 percent. You now add an additional $10 to the price of the item. To break even you have to charge $32. That is your real cost of this particular item. You determine that you want a 20 percent profit. You would then add an additional $6.40. You will, under this method, mark the price of the item to $38.40 in order to achieve your objectives.

Usually the charge for overhead assumes a normal production level and is based on your records of previous costs. However, during periods of rapid inflation, you have to be careful not to jeopardize your firm's financial position. Wherever possible, you should use current or future costs in establishing price. You also need to consider supply and demand and watch for the competition's attempts to undercut your prices. You might consider a low profit margin with the idea of having a higher profit on future servicing of the product or by increasing your sales volume. Expanding your share of the market and attempting to keep other potential competitors out of your market also can be smart moves. Your accountant can assist you in these analyses.

Incremental Analysis Pricing

Incremental analysis is pricing used when you have products that either compete with, or complement, each other. You can take into account the impact on total business operations that a new product may have. For instance, the new product may be competing adversely with another of the firm's products. It may, over time, require additional capital equipment or become costly to develop or buy. On the other hand, it could be complementary to another of the firm's products and could enhance sales of the other product dramatically, thereby increasing total profits. The way "Incremental Analysis" works, then, is to look at all these changes—anticipate disproportionate profits or costs—and adjust your prices accordingly. An example of this would be the following:

You feature a line of hamburgers at your fast-food franchise. You decide to introduce pizza. The pizza will require significant investment in new equipment. It may cannibalize your sale of hamburgers, or it may bring in families and associates of diverse tastes, finding common ground at your shop that provides a greater variety of food selections.

Cost of Producing the Product or Service

Cost, as has been stated earlier, is one of two influencing variables with which firms must deal in their determination of prices. It is the deduction of costs from total revenue that determines the firm's overall profitability. There are many different kinds of costs that a firm may consider. There are variable costs (the costs of production that vary as output varies), and fixed costs (those costs that remain constant irrespective of the level of output) such as rent, staff on fixed salaries, signs, and equipment leases.

When we speak of opportunity costs, we are generally referring to those alternative choices that could have been made, that would have resulted in different costs. For instance, if the resources of the firm had been used in the production of a different product, resulting costs may have differed. Another example of an opportunity cost would be a decision to not introduce products that require new equipment, but instead to invest that money in advertising current products. The decision would be based on a belief that there would be a greater increase in revenue in making one decision over the other.

Social costs are those which by their nature are not borne by the firm but by society at large. Social costs include the recycling programs that many companies have gone into, as well as adding biodegradable products for packaging.

Historical costs are those that have been borne in the past but which have no relevance to current decision making. Historical costs are those which financial analysts gather and record for financial statements.

Finally, there are explicit costs such as rent, materials, wages, interest, and so forth.

An accountant may view costs in slightly different ways than an economist would. For example, although historical costs are important to the accountant in record-keeping and financial statements, they may not be the total answer. The economist may consider that historical costs present too narrow a picture of the firm in decisions affecting production today and in the future. There may be, for example, implicit costs that do not involve actual payments but are, in effect, costs to the firm. These costs are not used in alternative ways or to produce alternative products. A clear example of an implicit cost may be the time and managerial effort given to a firm by a single owner/manager. That individual may very well pay himself/herself as owner/manager less than he could earn elsewhere. Assume for example that an owner/manager could, by working in a local corporation, earn $75,000 a year as manager, but in managing his/her own small business decides to take a salary of only $40,000. That $40,000 will be recorded by an accountant as managerial costs. An economist would look at the opportunity costs, i.e., would look at the differential, or $75,000, as being an implicit cost or an alternative cost. The economist's balance sheet may therefore differ from that of the accountant.

Premium Pricing and Value Pricing

If you have a product that does not have competition, such as the Burger King Whopper, you can charge a higher price than competitors in your market. This is generally described as premium pricing.

Value pricing is demonstrated by Don Wollan, Burger King franchisee in San Diego. Don highlights low-priced hamburgers in his direct mail advertising pieces. He prices these hamburgers significantly below competitors in an effort to develop trial, and thereby a new and enlarged customer base. His business has grown in terms of growth sales and profitability. It's the key to his marketing strategy.

When a restaurant owner sells a discounted hamburger, there is a strong likelihood he will make up any loss of revenue by selling additional items such as french fries, shakes, drinks, and desserts. The value-priced item could be designed to attract children and encourage their parents to make more expensive selections. Sometimes, though, value pricing doesn't work the way it's intended.

For example, Miguel Sherman, regional vice president of Super-Cuts, Inc., the highly respected haircutting franchise, recently opened two new SuperCuts stores in two similar communities in Southwestern Florida. Both communities had similar demographics, and the stores had like visibility and access. Both were heavily marketed on their initial opening by means of newspaper, direct mail, door hangers, and cable television. The advertising introduced the new stores with special introductory 50 percent pricing. As you might guess, business boomed. In one of the stores, the customer count was as high as some company stores had attained after two to three years in business. The problem was that by operating at full capacity at the discounted pricing, the company couldn't make any money. According to plan, prices were increased. In the one store, prices were returned to full price after the initial 30-day introduction. The result was a dramatic drop-off in clientele. In the second store, increased pricing was gradual, and designed to be implemented in three steps. The drop-off of customer base was gradual and less dramatic. The first increase brought a 5 percent loss of clientele. The second increase brought an additional loss of 10 percent. In addition, customers at this store were confused. Unlike the hamburger trade that might drop in on Friday evenings or Tuesday afternoons, haircut clients needed haircuts in a fairly routine manner. On each return to the shop, prices had changed. Many new customers were confused.

What Miguel learned is that value pricing had mixed results for the company. It brought in large numbers of new clients. Unfortunately, many of these new customers did not fit the SuperCuts profile. They were there merely to benefit from the low prices and had no product loyalty. When the price went up, they were gone. If value pricing has some benefit in developing new clientele, he determined that it is important to increase prices gradually over a prolonged period of time, so as not to lose the benefit of the initial advertising campaign.

There were some other negatives that had not been considered. The campaign was damaging to staff morale. The company had hired and trained many operators to service the large number of customers who initially frequented the shops. The operators were pleased with the numbers of clients and the volume of tips. Then these tips dropped off with the loss of customers. The loss of customers also brought shortened business hours for the staff. This resulted in unusually high staff turnover. If he were to do it over, Miguel's assessment is that he would not have introduced so large a discount as to cause so great an increase and then a possible drop-off of customers. Pricing closer to the standard price of SuperCuts might have resulted in initially attracting the more characteristic client of a SuperCuts shop.

Miguel Sherman had another good example of the impact of pricing. At one point, many SuperCuts shops in the U.S., both company and franchisee, raised prices from $6 to $8 per haircut. This dramatic increase of 33 percent brought a general drop-off in customers of up to 25 percent per shop. Areas impacted by poor economies and recession were especially hurt. Many of the franchisees opted to roll back prices. They found that they were able to recoup their clients. In one example, a store in an area with a particularly hard-hit economy was able to bring its price level down and increase its sales so significantly that their sales and volume of business are actually in the Top 10 nationwide.

My experience as a Weight Watchers franchisee was much the same. In running Weight Watchers of the Rocky Mountain Region, we made a strategic decision not to do discounting. Instead, we put the additional revenues into quality staff training, refurbishing the meeting locations, and other business-enhancing programs. On that basis, we were able to run a very successful operation.

After we sold the franchise to Weight Watchers International, discounting became the policy of the corporation. We believe that this stemmed from the company's extensive experience with the discounting of food products. We saw the volume of clients to Weight Watchers see-saw. Ups and downs in attendance were dramatic. People waited for discounting opportunities before they would join Weight Watchers classes. Higher volumes of business appeared to become increasingly dependent on discounting. The basis for this decision to discount becomes clearer when one understands that Weight Watchers International is owned by the H. J. Heinz Corporation. H.J. Heinz is one of the largest food producers and distributors in the world. When one realizes that Weight Watchers members traditionally buy the Weight Watchers food products, discounting makes more sense. H.J. Heinz corporation has done statistical assessments to ascertain the average number of food product purchases per new member to Weight Watchers classes. This translates to more dollars to the H.J. Heinz corporation, but not necessarily to the Weight Watchers franchisee.

My conclusion: value pricing works when there are other products that can be purchased alongside at full or premium pricing. Otherwise it appears to cause a long-term dependency on discounting, along with dramatic swings in business that precipitate staff morale problems, overall staffing problems, and that attract clients lacking in overall product loyalty.

Everyday Low Pricing

Thanks to the Walmart success story, the latest pricing strategy to emerge is that of everyday low pricing. In a recent article in *Advertising Age*,[3] everyday low pricing strategies have emerged as a pricing strategy to replace expensive promotions. John Martin, president of Taco Bell, a unit of Pepsico and one of the nation's largest and most successful franchisors, has vowed not to raise prices for five years.[4] Martin's decision is based on his philosophy that only quantum leaps in productivity will allow his operation to face the 1990s. The generally accepted norm for cost of goods sold in the food industry is 30 percent. That means for every dollar spent for fast food, you are actually getting about 30 cents in food.

To implement the strategy, Taco Bell has become a food assembler. It consigns to suppliers from outside virtually every other step in preparing the food. Meat and vegetables are delivered to the stores cooked, chopped, and ready for assembly in pre-fried shells.

The savings are 15 man-hours a day for a typical store. That money saved can be put back into food or pricing or promotion.[5] It also calls for fewer managers and supervisors.

There is another side to this picture of allowing outsiders to take over the production. New niche businesses arise. One young and promising franchisor is Dessert Cart. This company produces signature desserts for restaurants, creating a different specialty for each restaurant. Then they deliver these desserts on a regular basis to the restaurant. Changes in businesss philosophy that allow one company to grow very big also create new opportunities for niche businesses, some of which are now franchising.

Price Wars

One of the very risky arenas you could find yourself in is a price war. Although price wars can be a fact of life in the economy, they are usually based on the philosophy of pursuing market share at all cost.[6] The underlying purpose is generally accepted to be the desire to drive one's competition out of business. If you do not have deep pockets and get caught up in a price war, you can find yourself losing money on every sale, and you may ultimately find your business at risk.

If caught in this situation, contact your franchisor immediately for advice. Develop a strategy. Don't just react to your competition. Be proactive and prepared.

As you can see, there are a variety of pricing strategies. You must develop the philosophy that fits your business. You don't necessarily have to agree with you franchisor. I didn't agree with Weight Watchers International that discounting day in and day out was the way to sell this outstanding program. The franchisor cannot dictate pricing to you. This is an area where you do have some flexibility. Understanding the alternatives and applying the right one to your business can make a big difference in your total cost or profit.

ENDNOTES

[1] Michael D. Mondello, "Naming Your Price, Mini-MBA Pricing," *Inc.*, New York, NY, July 1992.

[2] Ibid.

[3] Julie Liesse and Judann Dagnoli, "Alternative Pricing Sets Off New Questions," *Advertising Age*, Chicago, IL, February 24, 1992.

[4] Bill Saporito, "Why the Price Wars Never End," *Fortune*, March 23, 1992.

[5] Ibid.

[6] Ibid.

PART THREE

Financial Management and Operations

CHAPTER 8

Controlling Costs

Most often we think about raising prices as the main way to increase profits. However, if you are in a competitive field, it may be wiser to consider the possibility of reducing your operating and overhead costs. This can be accomplished through improved control of your business costs. It also requires careful attention to each aspect of your business. For example, improvement of your record-keeping can be a way to better control the costs of operating your franchised business. In this chapter we'll look directly at cost management, and hopefully you'll walk away better able to reduce unnecessary expenses and implement cost-cutting procedures.

Fixed Costs

In your business, you're facing two kinds of costs. Let's start with fixed costs—those that remain constant at any range of operation. They are sometimes referred to as overhead costs. These include rent, insurance, executive wages, and some taxes. Your rent, for instance, stays the same regardless of production. The same is true of all fixed costs. If you have a team of executives and managerial staff members who are paid salaries, these salaries generally are not related to production. Of course, if production goes down, and looks as if it will plateau at a lower level than before, you may be forced to consider some salaried staff reduction. It is sometimes necessary to lower fixed costs, especially during reductions in production that appear that they will continue over a long period of time.

Some costs may be both fixed and variable. That is, depending on the volume of business, costs will rise. However, the increase in costs will not be at the same rate as the increase in operations. An example of a cost that is both fixed and variable is an electric utility service. There may be a minimum flat rate component and an additional amount that will go up after a certain kilowatt usage. All usage above that rate will bear additional charges. One scenario could be a company that has a basic fixed cost of $500 a month for electricity, and for that amount can produce 50,000 units of its product. However, the charge for electricity remains $500 whether production is zero or 50,000 units, and production above 50,000 units requires 100 kilowatts for each unit produced. Therefore, electricity can be both a fixed and a variable cost—a fixed cost for 50,000 units or less and a variable cost for all units above 50,000.

Telephone service generally has the same semi-variable cost. Variable costs are just that, they vary with the specific unit. If a widget requires a plastic lid that costs $1 per unit, the lid is a variable cost. That is, the money is only spent when the unit is produced.

Controlling Fixed Costs

Most economists predict slow growth and frequent, though unpredictable, downturns for the 1990s. Those companies that manage their costs and margins and that can anticipate adverse business conditions will be better able to survive through the decade. You should look at reducing your expenses not only to enhance profits, but also to focus your attention on the problems and the costs that are critical to your profitability during adverse times. These could include service to your customers, adequate lighting, attractive decor, maintaining your image, and other things that would be considered important to your customer base.

How do you know what is important to your customers? Ask them. Survey them. Don't guess. You could be wrong. And be sure not to let go of those services that are important to your long-term, competitive advantage. If you are a print franchise, it might be 24-hour service. If you are an automotive service franchise, it might be clean surroundings and amenities, such as spotless bathrooms. If you are a hairstyling franchise, it might be the need to update style photos on a regular basis.

It is becoming increasingly important to cut fixed costs. With that in mind, here are some specific instances where you might be able to reduce your company's fixed costs:

1. Replacing in-house departments with outside services, including maintenance, advertising, and public relations. Be aware, though, that once you transfer the responsibilities for a service outside the company (to free-lancers or independent consultants), you've lost a certain amount of control.

2. Changing sales compensation to full or partial commission. This changes the cost of sales from fixed to variable and makes results more measurable. An alternative could be to cover the poorest sales territories with commissioned personnel. Also, consider hiring outside contractors to do cleaning, alterations, drafting, landscaping, maintenance, and so forth.

3. Reviewing decisions as to whether it is more economical to manufacture or to purchase an item.

4. Leasing rather than buying property or equipment. This includes cars and trucks. Check this alternative carefully with your accountant, as tax implications will play a significant part in your decision.

5. Considering using public warehouses and common carriers rather than company-owned space and vehicles. In making this decision, be sure to evaluate all the costs involved in storage and shipping. These include personnel, benefits, equipment, and real estate costs including taxes, materials, and maintenance.

6. Arranging to have a "lockbox" at the bank close to where payers are bunched together. Let's say that your office is in Denver. You are doing business in Wyoming. Mail could be delayed. If that is the case, having a lockbox arrangement in a centralized part of Wyoming, e.g., Casper, could help to get those moneys collected and deposited more rapidly. All Wyoming money would enter the lockbox and be deposited in a

bank in Casper. The funds would then be wired to Denver. Although there is a cost for this service, it may be worth it. For example, if large amounts of money are being collected, getting it to the bank is important. An example of when this would work would be in the case of a master franchisee for a food operation. The quicker the money is deposited and working for you, the better off you are. A variation of this would be to set up an account with a large banking organization with branches in the cities that you do business. Again, getting the money deposited and working is essential.

7. Reviewing all activities related to your accounts receivable: telephone calls, insurance, rent and space utilization, use of copy machine, travel expenses, auto and truck leasing expenses, and so forth. There are companies that specialize in collections. They often can do a better job than your in-house staff for a lower cost. However, you do have to proceed with caution. Take care to investigate how such an outside service would treat your customer. You cannot risk that their personnel might alienate your clientele. You must do some checking before taking on such a service.

8. Reassessing your labor needs. Evaluate the ability to substitute part-time and temporary personnel for full-time employees. Part-time and temporary labor may be less expensive in both direct wage costs and in fringe benefits. Temporary workers, part-time help, students who can acquire valuable work experience, women with children at school, and retired workers may be interested in less than full-time work. Also, the costs of full-time employees may be cut by reducing turnover among your work force. They could experience the need to work, but find themselves stressed out. For example, a woman with small children at home may be able to juggle a part-time schedule. However, under a full-time schedule she could become stressed out or ill, and possibly quit because of the inability to balance all aspects of her life. The same could be the case for senior citizens, forced to earn extra income but finding themselves too stressed by full-time employment. If this is the case in your business, and you could find a place for part-time or temporary workers, it could help to cut re-training and recruiting costs.

9. Reviewing insurance policies to keep them current; you want to be fully, but not over-insured. Check deductibles. Perhaps you can live with a higher deductible. This could substantially lower your payments. Make sure all policies are packaged together. You may earn lower rates as a result of the packaging of insurance policies. Take advantage of your relationship with your insurance provider to evaluate your insurance coverage so that you are assured that you are getting the best rates. You may be able to comply with some accident avoidance procedures and thereby further lower your premiums.

10. Increasing the use of automation when appropriate. Perhaps you should be investing in computers, word processors, fax machines, and other office equipment that can maximize the productivity of office personnel.

Variable Costs

Variable costs are those that change in direct proportion to changes in production or sales (e.g., materials, commissions on sales, direct labor). This means that these costs are directly tied to production. There are fewer ways to control these costs, but they shouldn't be ignored.

Controlling Variable Costs

1. Watch travel expenses. Carefully review your travel expenses on a periodic basis. Consider using bed & breakfasts (B&Bs). Some of these are quite attractive, well maintained, offer excellent services, and add to the comfort of the business traveler. Look for bargain fares and coupon discounts. In recent editions of Gold C Coupon discount books, distributed in most cities, Continental Airlines offered a "dollars off" coupon. They had few restrictions, and it definitely applied to business travel as they didn't require Saturday layovers. United honored these coupons. Those businesses that took advantage of them, were able to cut the cost of travel.

2. Consider using conference calls or sophisticated conferencing services in order to avoid unnecessary and costly air travel.

3. Keep employees fully occupied during slack periods by having them perform outside contract work. This provides additional revenue for the company and keeps employees busy. However, when farming out valuable employees to other firms in need of their skills, you risk losing good employees. Caution is advised.

4. Implement controls on long-distance telephone calls. Some long-distance carriers will provide computer readouts on calls from specific phones.

5. Investigate substituting products and materials. In this day and age of innovation, there may be alternatives that will lower your costs.

6. Innovate in advertising. Perhaps you've been using television. You may find that taking some of your media dollars from television and placing it in radio would be beneficial.

7. Check into the benefits of joining a buyers club or shopping at an office discount store for supplies and equipment.

Staying on top of costs is essential. It is a way to increase profits without any additional sales. Often your franchisor will guide you in taking these cost-efficient steps. If not, it's important for you to take them. In one case, the franchisor had an elaborate proofing process that required an employee to show up three hours before opening to prepare the pizza dough. That added up to 21 hours of employee wages and benefits per week plus heat, air conditioning, lights, and related costs. The franchisee found a supplier for pizza dough, already proofed, that cost 10 percent more. This tradeoff eliminated substantial overhead cost. Evaluation of the above suggestions to maximize current resources and eliminate extraneous costs will help insure your business survival in the 1990s.

Some franchises have even organized around the concept of control of costs and increased business efficiency. One of these is the American Family Doctor.[1] New doctors have a certain number of options in initiating a practice—starting their own, joining a group practice, or seeking employment at a university or in a commercial group. Now they have a new choice—to become a franchisee with the American Family Doctor. This allows them to establish an independent practice. The franchise takes care of all of their administrative functions, freeing up the doctor to do what she has been trained to do—take care of patients.

Employee Leasing

Another cost-saving option for the 1990s is employee leasing, designed to cut benefit costs and reduce paperwork for employers. It also provides benefits to employees by permitting greater coverage to employees of smaller companies as well as lower deductibles. There are currently 1,300 companies doing employee leasing representing over one million leased employees.[2] These leasing companies are very helpful to small firms. There are, however, some pitfalls to be aware of. They are:[3]

1. The financial stability of the leasing firm. You want to avoid affiliation with a firm that could fail. You might be stuck with liability for the health claims and workmen's compensation claims.

2. You may have to comply with certain government regulations that normally exempt small businesses. An example would be the Americans with Disabilities Act. Firms of under 25 employees are exempt. Should you lease employees, you would no longer be exempt.

There are a few questions that you should be asking to ascertain your risk,[4] such as: How are health and worker's compensation plans managed? Is the leasing company self-insured? (This is declining due to regulatory pressure. Yet one-third of firms are still self insured.) Is the firm backed by an insurer? If yes, ask about the financial health of the insurer.

If the leasing firm has its accounts managed by a large insurer, it doesn't automatically mean the insurer in any way backs the leasing company. Also, beware of leasing companies that are promising too much for too little. It's likely that your fees will rise rapidly to realistic levels. Even worse, there is the possibility that they will be setting themselves up for failure. Nevertheless, for many companies, the leasing of employees has proven to be a beneficial arrangement. It is worth investigating.

Above all, good record-keeping is essential for tracking and evaluating costs. Ninety percent of all businesses that go out of business don't know why they did. Solid bookkeeping and record-keeping is a must if you have any intention of controlling your business costs.

ENDNOTES

[1] Janet L. Willen, *Nation's* "Doctors Examine Franchising," *Business*, June 1992, p. 65.

[2] Rosalind Resnick, "Leasing Workers," *Nation's Business*, November 1992, p. 20.

[3] Ibid.

[4] Ibid.

CHAPTER 9

Managing Your Money Effectively

Business money management is a very comprehensive subject. However, generally speaking, the franchise businessperson is not managing massive amounts of money. Having adequate cash flow, satisfactory profits, and sufficient working capital is such a desirable state to be in that it's easy not to think beyond this position. Nevertheless, it is important to move beyond this state of mind and to develop new focus regarding the management of money. In this chapter, we will address business money management from the franchisee perspective.

Working capital means the difference between current assets and current liabilities. We are going to make some concrete suggestions about the management of your assets and liabilities in a franchised business so that the cash and cash retention in your franchise are substantially improved. This area is seldom addressed by franchisors. If you're fortunate enough to have an all-cash business as fast-food franchises do, you can skip the Accounts Receivable and Cash Flow sections. Otherwise, all of these ideas should prove helpful.

129

When we refer to accounts receivable, we are referring to all outstanding billings to clients that have purchased your goods and services, yet to be paid. When referring to accounts payable, we refer to the money your firm owes to others for goods and services that you have purchased. You may consider accounts payable and accounts receivable to be passive aspects of your business. It's simple. You receive an order, then ship the merchandise. Then bill the company for the item or service, and wait for your payment. If the payment is late, you start sending out late statements. If you order an item, you wait for it to arrive. You receive the bill, and you pay for it. You may assume it's not a very dynamic part of your business. Right? WRONG!

You also may assume that this simple system of accounts payable and accounts receivable has worked well enough for years. But is this really the most efficient way for your franchise to operate? Look at it this way. Because of inflationary and recessionary pressures, hard times are upon us. These pressures will likely continue throughout the 1990s. Experts declare 10 percent of business failures were due to accounts receivable difficulties. A solid plan of cash flow management, designed to avoid cash shortages, is essential to good business management practices.

In times when cash is difficult to come by, or when interest rates are high, effective money management decisions that lead to improved cash flow can mean the survival of your business. The recommendations in this chapter can help get you through a cash crunch such as the one that occurred in April of 1980, when the prime rate climbed to 20 percent. Severe restrictions on lending were imposed by the Federal Reserve during this period. Credit appeared to dry up, especially for small businesses. This is an extreme example. Nevertheless, it is one to be heeded. The same lending crunch exists today for a totally different reason—the problems and insolvencies of many banks and savings and loans in the 1980s. The impact has carried into the 1990s and has resulted in tight money lending policies.

Accounts Payable

In managing your accounts payable, start with a plan. There are many steps that you can take to stretch out payments without affecting your credit ratings. Ask your creditors and suppliers for lines of credit. In a line of credit, the money is available in a set amount, as it would be for a loan. The key difference, though, is that the money does not have to be drawn until it is needed by your business. Since it is not drawn until it is needed, you are not paying interest on money that you are not using. Sometimes a line of credit made available by a supplier will be made available without interest. Another tactic is to ask for extensions in your periods of payment. If you cannot get a line of credit without interest, it is sometimes possible to negotiate an installment payment plan at favorable interest rates.

Another tactic is to ask suppliers to hold some of your inventory, and to only make partial shipments to you. Request partial billing along with the partial shipments. You benefit by having a predetermined, fixed price for the merchandise you require to do business. The supplier is guaranteed a large order. This can be a favorable business deal to both parties under certain circumstances. One area where this works especially well is in printing orders. There is hardly a franchised business that is without substantial printing requirements. It is cheaper for the printer and for the buyer to have items printed in large amounts. If the printing company is guaranteed a large sale, it may be agreeable to store the merchandise, assuming adequate space is available. The printer benefits by running the presses more efficiently, by processing larger paper orders at better prices, and through more efficient use of personnel. The buyer benefits with reduced merchandise costs, the need to pay for merchandise as it is required, as well as storage assistance. There are many parallel examples. For example, in fast-food franchises, we could be talking about customized napkins, paper plates, and cups. In automobile lube franchises, the items could be oil and filters. Evaluate your franchise and see if there are products that you require in large quantities.

Franchising also offers an added benefit in purchasing. The franchisor or a group of local franchisees can coordinate a large group purchase. The purchase could be a windfall to a supplier. This could lead to the supplier's cooperation in pricing, deliveries, storage, and in beneficial terms. It also could result in improved service.

Discount Billing and Letters of Credit

Take advantage of discounted billing whenever available. If a supplier will give you a 2 percent discount for paying a bill within 30 days, consider it a bonus. It is decidedly to your advantage to wait until the last possible moment within the 30-day period, then pay the bill and earn the 2 percent discount. That adds up to a hefty rate of savings of 24 percent a year for items ordered monthly. Use the money until the last possible moment, and then take full advantage of this additional money management technique.

You can also use a letter of credit with suppliers. A letter of credit is a guarantee from your bank that the funds will be available when needed. It is a letter that is put up by the bank on your behalf in lieu of bond. This was once only commonly used by large firms, but has become increasingly popular with small business owners and managers. Retail franchises can particularly benefit from this money management technique. If you use a letter of credit in dealing with your suppliers, it can give you an extended period of payment and assure some important guarantees for both parties. This can be very useful to a retail franchise, such as Wicks and Sticks or The Mole Hole.

For example, a retail franchisee orders a large shipment of Christmas gift items from a supplier 2,000 miles away. You may not know anything about the reliability of the supplier, but you do know that if the items arrive late and you miss the Christmas market, the merchandise is useless. Meanwhile, the supplier is insisting that the only way they will accept the order is if you pay in advance. In this scenario, a letter of credit is the ideal way of solving the impasse. Both sides get the security they require. The letter of credit guarantees full payment if the goods arrive on time. Both sides are assured that the factors most important to each are being met. You'll get the goods on time, or you don't pay. The supplier has guaranteed payment if they deliver in accordance with the contract. Another advantage for you is that no prepayment has been required by the seller. Therefore, your current funds can be put to alternative uses until the Christmas gift items are available for sale. This not only addresses your payables, but also directly results in improved cash flow.

There is one other payable to be considered—your income tax payable. Individual business owners and corporations are required by the Internal Revenue Service to make periodic installment payments based on estimated taxes for the year. Work with your accountant to be sure that this allocation is made.

Accounts Receivable

When you are on the other end, waiting for your bills to be paid, you can take a number of steps to avoid potential problems. First, recognize that unpaid billings are a major business problem. This is not as simplistic as it initially may sound.

There is a high cost to overdue accounts. An estimate from the accounting firm of Alexander Grant and Company indicates the following:

Past due status	Likely recovery (cents on the dollar)
30 days	.97
90 days	.90
120 days	.80
6 months	.67
1 year	.45
2 years	.23
3 years	.12

This chart can be shocking if you've never thought about it in these terms. Add the inflationary factors, the loss of interest, the lost use of the money, the reduced monetary value of late money, and most importantly the impact on cash flow, and you can see how substantially your business can be hurt by the slow recovery of accounts receivable.

James G. Seff, a C.P.A. in private practice in Denver, Colorado, has had extensive experience in working with franchises. He says "the process of credit and collection represent the ultimate realization of a sale. Without a systematized approach to the management of credit and collection, the continuity of a business can be severely impaired. The sale of goods and services is never a financial finality until cash is realized." That's a key message for those of you who manage franchises with receivables.

Start by understanding that the average business collects all of its receivables in 30 to 45 days. Now check this against your collection timetable. If it's not on track, the following are recommendations to address this situation:

1. Emphasis first should be placed on the collection of high dollar invoices, to increase overall cash flow. You also can bill for each shipment made as opposed to doing monthly billings.

2. You can time your billings to coincide with your customer's payment dates. If your customer states that bills are paid on the 10th of each month, be sure your bill is there before that date.

3. You can charge interest penalties to risky customers, or to those with histories of being substantially past-due on their payments.

4. You can carry bad debt insurance if it is available to your industry.

5. One way to handle customers who consistently pay late is to bill early. Notify customers that you are billing them 30 days in advance to give them sufficient time to process the invoices.

6. Picking up checks in person is a subtle way to avoid the "it's in the mail" routine.

7. Another, more direct, method is to provide disincentives for late payments. For example, rent paid on time is $3,000; rent paid after the 10th of the month is $3,300.

8. On service and consulting contracts, indicate that the work does not belong to the client until you are paid in full. This gives you substantive legal recourse.

9. Consulting franchises such as General Business Services or Total Business Systems have other options. Consultants can require a retainer. A retainer is a prepayment against which billings are made.

Keeping in mind that the people who owe you these moneys make up your customer base, it becomes apparent that collecting accounts receivable in a businesslike, expedient manner is essential to your business. Key markets, profitable customers, salable products and services, and developing and keeping key personnel are all important to the continued growth and development of a successful business, and all can be tied to efficient management of accounts receivable. Should you find it impossible to adequately monitor your accounts receivable, you can check into services available from accounting and other service firms.

You may find yourself extremely uncomfortable in working with overdue accounts. Be sure to get reliable, responsible, and competent help in this area. Also available to you is an accounts receivable analysis. It should give you the following information:

1. Which customers are buying, and which are not,

2. Which products and services are selling, and which are not,

3. Which territories and sales regions are the keys to your orders, and which regions are not producing,

4. Which salespersons are the producers in your organization, and which ones are being carried by the others,

5. Which accounts are truly profitable, and which ones are costing too much to service.

If Worse Comes to Worst

Once you identify perpetually delinquent customers and accounts too costly to service, you can take definitive steps to control this cost to your business. Make only partial shipments of the order, holding the rest of the order until payment is received. If necessary, even more drastic steps could be implemented. In a worsening situation, liens could be placed on the assets, members of the partnership, or the corporation. The accounts receivable also could be assigned to a collection agency. The problem with collection agencies is that it is not uncommon for them to split the collected amount 50-50. Since your profit margin is not generally as high as 50 percent, you will likely take a loss from using a collection agency. The loss is substantial when you consider that valued time and labor have been invested above and beyond the product or service sold. Nevertheless, there are times when it becomes necessary to accept the immediate loss to avoid a larger loss.

It is not always necessary to turn collection problems over to a collection agency. Your bank may maintain a collection service at a nominal fee or as a bank service. You can check into the availability of this service when determining which bank you'll do business with.

One study evaluated collection agencies that charge fees of between 30 percent and 50 percent of all bills collected. Firms in high tax brackets may find that the federal government can be more generous than the collection agency business. A table was developed that demonstrates the more efficient choice for a firm in the 35 percent marginal tax bracket.[1]

Collection agency discount rate	Efficient choice
30%	Use collection agency
33%	Makes no difference
35% and above	Deduct from taxes

If you face a consistent problem with collections, it would be wise to consult with your accountant to determine if it would be better to utilize the services of a collection agency or to write the losses off of your income taxes.

Another potential recovery method, available when it is economically feasible, is small claims court. In small claims court, you represent yourself without an attorney. However, each state has different limitations and regulations. It is important that you make a copy of every client check received. This will give you their banking source should the small claims court make a judgment in your favor.

Collecting on overdue accounts has to be considered a cost to your business. It is essential that you analyze, on a regular basis, the average costs of collection and assign them to the fixed costs of your business, either monthly or annually. Include a percentage of loss, known as a bad debt allowance, as a business cost. Ignoring these costs could cause serious cash flow problems. If your own creditors become impatient and unwilling to wait you out, a cash crunch can bring down your business in short order.

Cash Budgeting and Cash Flow

Cash budgeting refers to the preparation of cash flow statements. These statements usually are prepared by an accountant or by your financial officer and used to measure the changing level of cash during a specific period of time. It is an estimate of cash receipts and payments and is designed to specifically address the problem of having adequate cash on hand to meet business debts in a timely manner.

Many businesses run headlong into a financial crisis when they hit a cash flow crunch. That is, in spite of the apparent profits on the books, when the time comes to pay bills, through inadequate planning, there is a shortage of cash available to pay those bills. Although your business may appear profitable, you may find paying bills in the day to day becomes difficult due to cash flow problems. The first place to look for your problems is in your accounts receivable statement. Specifically, look for an excessive investment in your receivables.[2]

According to James Howard, Chairman of the Board of Asset Growth Partners, Inc., a New York City-based financial consulting firm for small businesses, "Small businesses focus on building sales, which is perfectly appropriate. But, it is not enough." You may have to look at accounts receivable as well as reducing expenses.

Here is how a cash flow problem works: You may estimate that it costs you $3,000 to produce 200 widgits per week, or $15 each. You may be assured that you have a market for the widgits that will bring you $4,000. Your potential profit is $1,000, and you feel you can run your business on that margin. On paper it looks perfect. The profit potential appears to promise you a successful business.

However, there's a major catch. Much of the expense has to be borne before any moneys come into the business. Raw materials, rent, utilities, labor, all require immediate payment. You can't risk being evicted, having your utilities shut off, or your staff seeking employment where they can be paid on a regular basis. Meanwhile, while all of these ongoing costs demand immediate payment, what is happening with your product sales? Perhaps those customers purchasing those widgits are not paying the bills as quickly as you'd like. As a result, receivables are coming in slowly. At the same time, your creditors are closing in on you. Figure 9-1 is an example of the cash flow cycle of a business.

This problem, where there is a time lapse between production and collection, can cause a business to go under when it becomes severe. You must negotiate an adequate line of credit ahead of time, or you must come up with another way of keeping a good cash flow situation. For instance, if you're having collection problems, get on the phone with the payer. Negotiate terms. Get some cash in. Go out

Figure 9–1
The Cash Flow Cycle of a Business

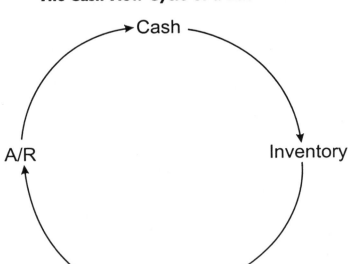

and visit the business, if at all possible, in order to initiate collections. Start billing twice a month if necessary rather than only once.

If you have weekly payroll switch to bi-weekly. If your payroll is bi-weekly, switch to a monthly payroll. This permits less frequent tax deposits, and longer use of your cash.

Consider dropping late-paying customers. Discuss this first with these customers. They may be using you as a means of aiding their own cash flow.

Most importantly, draw up a plan of action and stick to it. Maintaining a solid line of credit and a good business relationship with your banker should be a major consideration throughout this process.

You may notice that you may have to be tough with those owing you money, while at the same time trying to get the cooperation of those to whom you owe money. It may seem to be a double standard, but it is good business savvy to put yourself in the best cash flow position possible.

Another way to put yourself in the best cash flow position is to once again look at the use of a line of credit. A line of credit, as was recommended in Chapter 3, is frequently preferable to a loan. If you assure your line of credit at the higher end of your budgeted cash flow requirements, the money is then available as it would be for a loan. However, the money does not have to be drawn until needed. Therefore, you're only paying interest on the money you require at the time. Theoretically and statistically, all money requirements do not become due at the same time. At times, when there is a solid cash flow in the business, little would be drawn down; at other times, substantial amounts would be needed. The advantage is obvious. You only are paying interest on the moneys you are using. Keep in mind, interest is a cost to your business. You should not be paying this cost other than when it is absolutely necessary.

Cash Management

When times are good, the results of poor cash management may not be felt. However, when times are not so good, and when margins are poor, you will not only feel the pinch, your business may fail. It's very important to consider cash management a basic business strategy that should be included in your business plan. This section deals with specific cash management tools that can be implemented in a number of franchised businesses. Even the area of investing your money calls for a little stretching of your imagination. The goal is to get as great a return on your money as you can while keeping it accessible.

Compensation

Evaluate salaries and payment schedules in your company. Talk to other franchisees and definitely seek out the experience and knowledge of your franchisor. Check that you're not employing too much staff. Be sure scheduling is evaluated and that you are maximizing personnel at peak periods and not at off hours. Check that salaries are competitive with the industry, or with salaries in your town, city, or community. Evaluate the benefits that your employees are receiving; are they fitting their personal needs? Talk with your staff; survey them. See what the people working for you perceive to be valuable.

If you're considering a move, find out if the location would be compatible with the needs of your current employees.

Get employee involvement. Have staff members write out job descriptions, responsibilities, and indicate areas where they would be interested in adding responsibilities. Locate duplication. Gauge staff productivity. In very small companies, it may mean checking with every employee. In larger companies, it may mean getting the information from managers.[3]

Purchasing and Inventory Management

This area is so important to your cash management we have allocated a whole chapter (See Chapter 10) to it. If you are in an inventory-intensive business with major purchasing responsibilities, be sure that the responsibilities are carefully delegated and carefully monitored by appropriate management.[4]

Tracking

After you have your business plan in place and operating, it is essential to implement controls—that is, a tracking methodology to alert you when you are off course. Among these recommendations for tracking are the following:

1. Make sure only a few people handle cash.

2. Set up procedures to make them accountable.

3. Require invoices and purchase orders before issuing checks; informal procedures leave you vulnerable.

4. Limit the number of people who can authorize expenditures.[5]

Investing in Your Business

One of the first areas you should consider investing in is new equipment that could make you more competitive, more efficient, and more productive, or in real estate improvements. Another investment area is expanding through the acquisition of another company that is undervalued. If there would be a company that could be managed efficiently along with yours, it would be well worth considering. If your business is already a profitable one, you may be subsidized in your purchase of another business by current tax laws. Check this with your accountant.

Investing in Your Employees

Your employees are the backbone of your business. It's important to look closely at matters that affect them. For instance, your money management should include concern over the cost of employee turnover. Do a six-month study of all employees who left and why. Determine if you could have prevented the person, or number of employees, from leaving through a change in policy or some other way. Even without statistics, you can evaluate whether your turnover is too high. Then evaluate the cost of training new personnel.

Perhaps you have evaluated the turnover of personnel in your company and have the figures to compare it to the industry as a whole. This is not always possible, but in a franchise it is more likely to be possible. You have a team of fellow franchisees in the same business. They will benefit equally from such a comparison. Take advantage of being a franchisee. This is an opportunity not to be taken lightly.

You may find that you have been losing key personnel, and that it is hurting you financially, for reasons that may be possible to improve or change. Most likely you will find that even small changes can improve morale substantially. Consulting with your employees may raise their self-esteem and make them feel valued. That, in itself, is important in reducing employee turnover. Managers sometimes forget that the esteem level of employees is very important to the welfare of the company. Valuable contributions to the efficiency of the company come from employees who feel they have a vested interest in the company's success. Sometimes employees place "being a part of the company" ahead of salary and benefit concerns. And conversely, employee dissatisfaction—whatever the reason—can hurt your company.

It takes time, and that time translates into money, for management to discuss company conditions with employees. However, it is money well spent. If you are experiencing employee dissatisfaction, it is possible that your productivity levels will be down, morale will be low, turnover will be high—and your overall costs will increase.

To improve the situation, it is a wise move on your part to address staff needs.

It also may serve your company well to consider profit sharing and pension plans. These may be the more complex types governed by the ERISA act and the Keogh and IRA plans. ERISA stands for Employee Retirement Income Security Act and was enacted in 1974. It usually, but not always, is reserved for larger businesses. One of the important aspects of these plans is that they serve as a forced savings, on a tax-free basis, for employees. Employees see a growing fund that increases their personal identification with the goals of the company. Seeing that they're getting a percentage of the profit, and that their retirement needs have been partially addressed, may substantially reduce your employee's stress levels. This, in turn, may cause their productivity to increase.

Other employee benefits you might consider are medical and dental coverage, which go a long way toward easing financial pressures on employees while providing a better atmosphere for higher productivity.

Managing Advertising Funds

In some businesses, particularly in franchises, another effective means of money management could be the establishment of an in-house advertising agency. This is especially desirable when your franchisor supplies you with camera-ready ad copy for newspapers, or commercial copy ready for radio and television stations. If you develop an in-house agency, you can effectively keep the 15 percent that is allocated to an advertising firm when it places media advertising.

However, this is not always a wise move. The services of an advertising agency are in the area of professional art production, copy production, media selection and placement, troubleshooting, and other related advertising programs. In some situations, the small businessperson is talented in these advertising areas and can handle the responsibility. There is a lot of time and energy involved in doing your own advertising, and if you have a flare for this area or can hire someone who does, you can realize substantial savings.

You also can consider hiring the services of a free-lancer in your community. Even in a small city, there are usually free-lance services for hire in all aspects of advertising. Although many of these moves save money, you do not want to sacrifice quality. Consult with your franchisor to assure that you are making the best decision for your franchise.

Managing Money Through Bank Services

The services that a bank can provide to your business is another area to evaluate. Many of these services could be financially advantageous to a franchise. We already have talked about three of these—loans, lines of credit, and letters of credit. In addition, some banks have extensive seminar programs at very reasonable costs, which may include such subjects as "Tools for Financial Planning," "Starting Your Own Business," "Financial Planning and Budgeting," or "Real Estate for the Beginning Investor." In addition to seminars, extensive lists of consumer and business-oriented booklets are available from the Bank of America, Avco Financial Services, and other banking and financial institutions.

Some banks make business consultants available to customers. These consultants can include economists, accountants, marketing experts, and tax attorneys. Banks also can be helpful in the area of real estate. Since many real estate closings take place at bank offices, there are often highly trained, knowledgeable persons regarding real estate available for consultation and advice. They should not or cannot replace your accountant or lawyer, but they can be helpful in the planning stages of any business moves. They can recommend the best sources of surveys, appraisals, location and site analyses, and, of course, the best ways to structure the financing.

Some banks have accounting and payroll services, which are often computerized, as well as general ledger and balance sheet preparation and analysis.

Payrolls handled by computer can be convenient and can save time and money. This is especially true of accounting fees, since much of the data can be tallied inexpensively and reported regularly to employees and management. Bank payroll services may also make immediate monthly, quarterly, and annual reports. There are also excellent and inexpensive payroll computer software programs available on the market. Check them out. They permit in-house staff to manage payroll input. From this input, the program prepares sophisticated and required payroll reports. The result is reduced accounting costs without sacrificing quality.

Using a Financial Consultant

There are many other money management concerns for small businesses. Examples are whether to rent, to build, or to buy a building; tax benefits; and choice of location for future flexibility and growth projections. Each business manager must recognize that, besides the everyday, efficient management of their business, there is a need to efficiently manage their money. If you are paying excessive interest or if you are missing out on tax benefits, you are wasting money. Poor personnel management may cause you to re-think your policies. You may be losing dollars in training time or in scheduling.

You may find it advantageous to hire a financial consultant to do an evaluation of your business as it moves through different phases of growth. As the external and internal situations related to the business change, there is a need for the business to change, too.

Making Your Cash Work for You, Short-Term

A registered investment advisor can help you to invest short-term cash more wisely. There is even a franchise that specializes in doing just this. Creative Asset Management, based in Iselin, New Jersey, specializes in fee-based investing. They help clients put their excess cash to work in no-load or non-commissionable products, so that 100 percent of a client's money is at work for her.

If you are on your own, the first rule is to be sure to deposit your checks daily into money market accounts. An extra day or two of interest every week can add up to a substantial amount of money over a year. Tax anticipation notes are another place to put one's moneys. These are short-term notes issued by municipalities. Besides somewhat better yields, they are tax-free. This is a particularly good short-term investment for franchises in higher tax brackets.

Commercial paper is the short-term, unsecured promissory note of a large, creditworthy corporation. These are issued by the corporation in order to raise working capital. Minimum investments are $25,000. Notes are usually sold on a discount basis and pay face value at maturity, which varies from one to 270 days. *Industrial paper* is issued by major industrial firms through banks and brokers. Maturities are geared to the industrial firm's needs; the investor's selection of maturities is subject to market availability. Yields are higher than on finance paper.

Finance paper is issued by major sales financial companies and some large bank holding companies. Investors have the option of specifying the issue date and maturity date so funds will be available when needed. This is a major benefit to the investors, allowing for flexibility.

If you have $100,000 or more, you can place it in a commercial bank or thrift institution at a negotiated rate of interest. These are know as *negotiable certificates of deposit* or *CDs*. The key is to shop around for the highest yield on your deposit. The $100,000 that you use can be combined from several sources, such as savings, or profit sharing and pension funds, to achieve this higher rate. The new rate can be substantially above current interest rates for standard accounts. There is usually a 30-day minimum for these moneys. Another benefit is that the FDIC and FSLIC insure these accounts for the total $100,000. This is important because of the shaky situation of many banks and savings and loans in the U.S.

Another variation into the money market field is *tax-free money market funds*. These are made up of public housing authority instruments. The initial investment range is from $1,000 to $10,000 depending on the fund, and they currently yield about 5 percent. Although this is not currently a high yield, they may be watched as a potential investment.

Making Your Cash Work for You, Longer-Term

Considered among the best and safest investment opportunities are *U.S. Treasury bills*. They are the equivalent of cash because, in an active secondary market, they are bought and sold over the counter. They can be considered a highly liquid investment, readily converted to cash. They are auctioned on the basis of three-month, six-month, and twelve-month maturities. The three-month and six-month maturities are auctioned weekly; the twelve-month on an every-four-week basis. They are sold at a discount and redeemed at face value. There is a minimum face value of $10,000.

If you want to preserve and maintain a high degree of liquidity, you can invest in *short-term Treasury bills*. These are now available for a $1,000 minimum investment and come highly recommended as a secure hedge against inflation. *U.S. Treasury notes and bonds* also are available in minimum investments of $1,000. Treasury notes mature in periods of one to 10 years, and pay interest semiannually by means of coupons that must be clipped and redeemed. Treasury bonds mature in five to 30 years.

There are also many *federal agency securities* available. They have been created by Congress to finance various segments of the economy. Some are guaranteed or sponsored by the U.S. Treasury, but most are not. Therefore, the yield is usually higher than direct Treasury obligations. Examples are Federal National Mortgage Association (FNMA, popularly known as Fannie Mae), or Federal Home Loan Mortgage Corporation (FHLMC, or Freddie Mac). Other agencies deal in agricultural credit. You can check with a reliable stock brokerage firm for full information on these agency obligations and a current listing of those that are available.

Summary

As a franchisee, you have an advantage over other small businesses. Although it is unlikely that your franchisor would become involved in the money management of your franchise, you have a team of fellow franchisees in the same business situation. You are a member of a team with similar goals and objectives, as well as like problems. Together, you can benefit from skilled and appropriate professionals who can assist you in establishing and implementing a cash management plan designed specifically for your franchise. With your fellow franchisors, you could share the costs of tailor-made programs for cash management. Remember, this is not to be postponed. The benefits go directly to your bottom line.

ENDNOTES

[1] Bruce R. Siecker, "Managing Customer Credit," *Drug Topics*, October 1, 1979, p. 38.

[2] Bryan E. Milling, *Cash Flow Problem Solving*, Chilton Book Company, Radnor, PA, 1981.

[3] Roberta Maynard, "Smart Ways To Manage Cash," *Nation's Business*, August 1992, p. 43.

[4] Ibid.

[5] Ibid.

CHAPTER 10

Purchasing and Inventory Management

Purchasing is an area of significant importance to the franchisee, yet it's often an area that is ignored. In many cases your franchisor will have a purchasing system in place. Many franchisors have complete purchasing packages designed to initiate operations with a minimum of brain damage. The specifications are included in the operations manual or an auxiliary manual. Approved suppliers are indicated, along with addresses, phone numbers, and contact persons. The franchisor already may have negotiated preferential pricing. If so, this pricing would be available to you, along with required items and pricing schedules. In addition, these franchisors take the responsibility of regularly updating this information.

There is a legal prohibition against "tying." This means that a franchisor cannot control an item required by the franchisee and that is readily available in the open market. Because of this prohibition, most franchisors will not supply required items to the franchisee, and they maintain the independence of the approved suppliers.

It would be wonderful if all franchisors orchestrated purchasing opportunities, but that doesn't always happen. In this chapter, we'll go through some steps designed to better equip you to handle purchasing should you find yourself on your own.

The Purchasing Process

Just as you have been encouraged to develop a marketing plan for your franchise, it will serve you well to develop a purchasing and inventory control plan. This could readily be included as a part of your overall business plan. Not controlling your purchasing and inventory can leave you highly vulnerable to unplanned purchasing.

This can come by way of telephone solicitations. Develop a high resistance level to telephone sales pitches. Often, peddlers of specials in office supplies will come by way of a telephone solicitation. Check these out before ordering. Find out what the cost of the item is, and if it can be refused and returned if it doesn't meet expectations. Protection is needed as the items sometimes turn out to be substandard and therefore no bargain at all.

An important policy approach in purchasing is to seek commitment to long-term price guarantees that protect you against rising prices. These are not always available, but at times can be successfully negotiated. If your supplier is experiencing competitive pressure, you may be in a position to tie down prices for extended periods of time, assuring control and stability in the process.

Factors That Influence Purchasing

Special factors influence purchasing by the franchisee. These could include anticipation of strikes, gas shortages, weather problems, and Christmas slowdowns. Some industries even shut down in unison for two or three weeks at a set time each year. Other businesses take inventory at year end, and there is a production-shipping slowdown during this period. It would be wonderful if your franchisor would direct you in these matters. However, if the franchisor does not provide this information, it is your responsibility to understand the particular industry factors that relate to purchasing. Remember that this information may, at times, be critical.

Determining Needs

The first step in your plan would be to determine your purchasing requirements. The following is an example of a start-up franchise equipment and supply list of a sign manufacturing franchise. If you were to purchase such a franchise, your operations manual might provide such an outline as follows:

- High-speed vinyl cutting machine
- 486/33 megahertz IBM-compatible computer
- 120 megabyte hard disk drive
- 1.2 megabyte floppy disk drive
- VGA color monitor
- Flatbed scanner
- 48-inch plotter/cutter with knife and pen
- Vinyl
- Transfer tape
- Banners

Specific brands may be preapproved by the franchisor. It is more likely minimum quality standards will be defined.

In running a Weight Watchers franchise, I had an operation that spanned four states. Within those states, I had to supply over 200 classes conducted weekly. Some of the meetings were held in locations that were totally allocated to Weight Watchers. We called these "Centers." Others were held in churches, schools, community centers, and the like. These had to be supplied in on-site secured storage. Besides master purchasing and inventory storage, each site had to maintain an inventory such as the following:

- Permanent items:
  - Medical scale(s)
  - Date stamps & stamp pad

  - Adjustments to weigh members of 300+ pounds
  - Pens/pencils
  - Night deposit bags/deposit slips
- Temporary:
  - Membership books
  - Diet books and updates
  - Maintenance plans and updates
  - Food diaries
  - Inventory supply forms
  - Financial reporting forms
  - Mailing envelopes

Locations, depending on the number of participants, had to maintain a sufficient inventory in order to operate. If you were in Greybull, Wyoming, you had to have sufficient supplies. You were hundreds of miles from a central office. No help or direction came from the franchisor. As franchisees, we were on our own to determine what we needed and when we needed it, and just how we were going to get it there.

In each case, as a franchisee, you must determine your own supply needs. If you are a food franchisee, you require fresh food on a regular basis. Creative Croissants, a restaurant franchise, has addressed this creatively. They contract with a local bakery or develop their own commissary to bake and freeze food items. Then they are baked fresh on the premises.

In a recent *Fortune* magazine article on the subject of inventory, it stated "too much inventory might get you chewed out, too little-might lose you your job."[1] As a franchisee, you won't lose your job. However, it may cost you some of your profit.

Selecting and Contacting Suppliers

It is beneficial to have two or three suppliers rather than just one. Relying solely on one supplier can be risky. Of course, if it's is an item of minimal importance to your business, having one supplier can simplify things. It is probably less expensive to do business this way. But when it comes to an essential item, a disaster could strike your business if that one supplier is having internal problems. Whether it's a fire or natural disaster, or a death or divorce in the supplier's family, it can affect your business. It could be vital if your access to a critical item is interrupted. It is best to be in a protected position when it comes to essentials. Get more than one supplier for critical items.

Accepting Bids

If your franchisor has negotiated prices for you, your immediate reaction to the bidding process is that it is irrelevant and uncomfortable. It was my experience, that with my franchisor based in New York and my operations based in the Rocky Mountain Region, it was most definitely to my benefit to learn about bidding. Because the Rocky Mountain area is not union-intensive, it was definitely a good idea to go out and to seek bids in pursuit of lower prices.

When your franchisor has provided you with an approved supplier list, most franchise agreements give you the right to submit other suppliers for approval. There is a process to follow, and the process usually is spelled out in your franchise agreement. It may require making a submission in writing naming the supplier and giving the address, phone number, contact person, and specifications of the item that you wish to purchase from another source. Remember, denial by the franchisor cannot be arbitrary. There are legal precedents protecting you in this case. Franchisees frequently indicate that franchisors are very supportive and will assist you with local suppliers.

In one situation, a franchisee advisory council negotiated a national automobile insurance program. To the vast majority of franchisees, especially those based in major cities, it was very beneficial. However, some franchisees, especially those based in areas where automobile insurance costs were generally low, were able to negotiate better local contracts.

In other cases, national suppliers may provide better prices. However, when you add shipping costs, delays, and the lack of local service, it can be to your advantage to deal locally, even at slightly higher prices.

Once you have determined your needs, you should put them in writing. You want to know what it is you want, the specifications, the quantity, and how often you'll require delivery. Then when you submit these items for bids, the responses you get will allow you to compare apples and apples. If you speak in generalizations, you risk bids that are apples and oranges.

Remember that you will be evaluating more than pricing in this process. Some of the other things that you'll look at in the bidding process are as follows:

1. The financial stability of the supplier

2. Billing terms

3. Dependability (check references)

4. Supplier practices and policies in case of damaged or substandard merchandise

5. Supplier policy and ability to repair items

6. Delivery policies and costs

7. Delivery schedules

8. Product variety

9. Willingness of supplier to store excess merchandise

As you can see, the bidding process is more complicated than it might initially appear. Be assured, it can readily be mastered and can help put you in control of the required purchasing for your franchise.

Prices

There can be significant variances in supplier prices. This is an extension of the bidding process. As a Weight Watchers franchisee, we were responsible for leasehold improvements and interior design on our center locations. We frequently had the added responsibility for heaters and air conditioners. In a crisis, such as the heater breaking down at 20-degree temperatures, you lose the flexibility to get bids and compare prices. Business interruption is frequently more costly than price differentials. However, in most cases, you are afforded the opportunity to get appropriate bids. You will find, as I did, that prices can vary considerably.

Bidding affords you the opportunity to compare prices and get the best possible deal. It gives you negotiating power, and empowers you to negotiate with some element of control over prices. If you know what you want, how much you need, and when you want it, you generally will be able to get the best price available.

All is not done, however, when the deal has been made. Periodically check on the price versus the quotation. Some suppliers will raise their prices without notifying you, and the new price may not be a price you're willing to pay. If the price has changed, you might want to go shopping again. One caution: if the person in your company who pays the bills is not the one who negotiated the price, a price change or an overcharge could result. You need to make sure this doesn't happen. Good in-house communication is essential.

Be sure to insist on written quotations with terms specified. After a solid, working relationship with a supplier is established, you may want to conclude future agreements with nothing more than a handshake. However, we recommend that, in all new purchasing agreements, the quotations and terms be put in writing to avoid potential problems. And keep these quotes filed where they are readily accessible.

It is often wise to buy in quantity, and, when possible, to have the supplier store the merchandise for you. This can be a very favorable situation to both parties. As mentioned earlier, with a large printing order, once the printer has set up the presses, printing in bulk is beneficial and can reduce cost significantly. It also allows for the efficient use of certain specialized printing presses. The guaranteed sale could offset storage costs to the printer. If you needed 20,000 of an item per month, ordering 100,000 and requesting shipment of 20,000 per month at the 100,000 price could be a satisfactory arrangement for both parties. Don't be discouraged if the first, second, or third supplier turns you down. Be tenacious. Find the one whose needs correspond to yours. There may be a supplier out there with excess storage space who is more than willing to conclude a deal that fits your needs.

Purchasing Staff

The purchasing agent for your franchise should not be viewed as office personnel, remote from operations. This could be a costly error to your success. If your franchise is not big enough to have a purchasing agent, we recommend that the person doing your purchasing understands how the product is to be used as well as how it works. In the printing field, for instance, an understanding of the different kinds of ink and paper (for example, its quality and thickness) and how they relate to the presses could help reduce wasted time and error. Training the purchasing agent is a worthwhile investment. It could save many unnecessary costs and reap many benefits. Each franchise must recognize its own needs relative to the goods purchased. Solid systems of communication among key employees facilitate the availability of marketable products at competitive prices. It is always wise in franchising to remember that you are not alone. Your franchisor or your fellow franchisees may stand ready to work with you to develop a purchasing staff training manual. The cost of such development is shared. Group knowledge is tapped into. Each participating franchisee is strengthened with the resulting training manual in hand.

Bartering

One other creative approach to purchasing is bartering. There are established retail and wholesale barter exchanges that can help you stretch your dollars. In an article in the June/July 1991 issue of *Franchise Update* magazine, I described how corporate barter could be used effectively in franchising from the franchisor perspective. However, it also can be used readily by many franchisees. If, for instance, you owned a print shop or a restaurant, you could make your services available for barter credits. If you run an auto service franchise or a dry cleaning franchise, you again have services to be made available. You then have credits available to purchase accounting services, legal services, advertising, and other products and services that you would require in the day-to-day operation of your business. There are many approaches to improving purchasing techniques and inventory storage. These considerations deserve a place in your operational plan. ITEX is one of the largest retail barter companies. It is also a franchise. You likely would find an understanding and supportive franchisee at ITEX to help you establish a barter account.

Controlling Inventory

Inventory can make up a major portion of cash outlays to many franchised businesses. If you are a USA Baby franchise specializing in retailing baby furniture, your entire business is inventory-based. If you are a Pizza Hut restaurant franchise, the freshness and perishability of your inventory are paramount to your success. Whatever your franchise, you have inventory of one type or another to contend with. Inventory is a business cost. Efficiency in controlling inventory goes to the bottom line. You are directly rewarded for control in this area.

Recognize Inventory Costs

Recognize all costs involved in inventory. Some may turn out to be hidden. Keep in mind that every dollar tied up in inventory is unavailable for any other purpose required by the company. It costs money to maintain inventory, as well as to produce or purchase it. Some of the costs associated with maintaining inventory include transportation, theft prevention, warehousing, insurance, guards, and obsolescence, as well as the lost opportunity to invest the capital tied up in the inventory.

Storage of excessive inventory is especially costly. Not only is there a risk of the product becoming outdated through newer technology, there is a risk of a reduction in the quality of the item. There is also a risk of damage; the longer many items are stored, the more many of them deteriorate. Some have a built-in shelf life. Others can become obsolete due to technological changes.

Despite these cautions, there are also benefits to larger inventories. They can insure that you can meet consumer needs immediately. In times of escalating costs, inventory bought at lower prices and larger volumes either can be sold more competitively or more profitably. These tradeoffs must be evaluated by each franchisee in her own field. Be sure to evaluate the required time for delivery of the item, quantity price reductions, cost, and availability of storage. There is the associated risk of the item becoming outdated, the quality possibly deteriorating during storage, and the general risk of damage to the merchandise itself.

Storage of inventory and ordering also relates to the rate of sales. If you sell an average of 100 toasters a month, but in the month prior to Christmas you sell 300, half of which tend to be deluxe models, you may find that distorts the average.

A careful evaluation of rate of inventory turnover is always essential. Many retail businesses sell as much as one-third of their annual inventory just prior to Christmas. Other businesses have to be equally concerned with the rate of sales. A sporting goods store most likely will not be able to move skis during the summer, unless a customer is headed for the Andes Mountains in Chile or Argentina. However, now, with a large availability of indoor tennis clubs, along with winter breaks in the weather, and follow-the-sun vacations, tennis rackets and clothes may sell all year long. In most businesses, franchises included, there is seasonal variability. Goods and services will sell at different rates in June than in January. It's up to you to track your sales and to be prepared for the variance.

If shipping is a major expense, see if the item can be packaged with lighter materials, without increasing risk. This can result in substantial reductions in shipping costs. If you are ordering custom-made items, it would be advisable to investigate if there are standard-sized substitutes available that could serve the purpose. Standard-sized items are generally manufactured in larger production runs. This often means greater demand, which adds up to lower unit costs.

Special Insurance for Inventory Protection

Have a system established so that all shipments are checked for damage on delivery. This protects you and the shipper of the merchandise. There is likely to be insurance on the shipment. Claims can be made immediately and generally will hold up. Delays could cause disallowance of the claim.

Kim Carl, a Pak Mail franchisee from North Charleston, South Carolina, discovered a cost-saving insurance measure. She found that during the Christmas season, heavy volume caused the backing up of packages on-site. Her normal insurance policy worked throughout the year, but at this high-volume shipping period, she was totally under-insured. The carrier was not responsible for the package until it was removed from her premises. Her remedy was to obtain a special policy for this short period of time. The cost of replacing missing merchandise, should it be stolen or damaged, could have put her out of business. Nevertheless, she didn't need to carry the higher level of protection throughout the year. Should you have peak periods of vulnerability, be sure to talk with your insurance agent to protect yourself in a cost-effective manner.

Inventory Control

Have the right quantity of inventory on hand. This is the cardinal rule of purchasing. If you run out of merchandise, you run the risk of losing sales or making your customers unhappy. If you have too much, it will reduce your cash flow, which is a risky position for a franchisee. An analysis of flow of inventory, month by month, is necessary. If you run primarily a service franchise with relatively few items to inventory, a general analysis and an order plan are probably satisfactory. If you are in the business of giving seminars, such as the Success Motivation Institute franchise, you may determine that you need 1,000 seminar brochures per month and 500 packets of materials. You may find printing these in orders of 2,500 is more cost efficient, as it permits periodic updating of material. If you determine it takes one to two weeks for delivery of printed matter, for instance, orders on brochures could take place when there are 600 in stock, and orders of packet materials when there are 300 in stock. However, if you determine, for instance, that January and February are your busiest months, inventories may be replaced at different and higher figures during these peak-use months. Learn the variables as they relate to your franchise. The time will be well invested.

Use Computers for Inventory Control

As inventories grow and become more complex, it may be wise to invest in a small business computer. A computer may help you effectively analyze your inventory, move products that have limited shelf life, order more appropriate items at the right time, and help in the immediate analysis of cost per item. It also could help you if you're planning to shift into other areas of sales. If you are in the business of bidding jobs, you could use the computer analysis of inventory as a contributing factor in the bidding process.

Computers have influenced the methodology for tracking inventory. In past years, what is known as the Periodic Inventory System was the more popular system. In this system the cost of goods sold and the inventory balance are updated at the end of an accounting period when an inventory is taken. This largely has been replaced by the Perpetual Inventory System. In this system, a running and continuous record that tracks inventory and cost of goods sold is maintained on a regular basis. Computerization has made the latter feasible and economical.

PC magazine did a study of LAN inventory software. The study evaluated and compared inventory software. Most of the software programs were PC-compatible on 80386 processors with 4 MB of memory. This type of PC is relatively inexpensive today.

Some of the software is available for networked computers. This means you could tie into multiple business outlets, or into your franchisor. The result in both scenarios could be more efficient inventory control and purchasing.[2]

If your franchisor has not provided you with an inventory control system, there is still no excuse for not having one. There is sophisticated and flexible computer software available in the market at reasonable cost. Some of it is directly tied to your cash register. As sales are made, inventory reports are produced. In some cases, these reports trigger automatic purchasing orders. The sooner that you incorporate a system appropriate to your franchised business, the better able you will be to control inventory and purchasing. This is a perfect opportunity if you have a Franchisee Advisory Council. This could be an excellent group project. Allocating resources to develop efficient inventory control and purchasing practices would be time and money well spent.

Restocking

Consider stocking up on certain inventory items before price increases. This, of course, would depend on having adequate storage space. You could possibly negotiate a large purchase with graduated shipments. For example, if notified in February that prices of toasters will increase by 10 percent on all purchases after March 15, it might be possible to negotiate the purchase of 1,200 toasters. You could arrange for 100 to be delivered each month at the old price. Remember, your figures showed you will need 100 toasters per month and

300 before Christmas. The upfront purchase commitment could possibly assure you the lower price. That added negotiation, successfully concluded, could increase your annual profits.

The Bigger Picture

Franchises vary significantly as to the importance of inventory control. A franchise like Creative Asset Management, the only investment advisory franchise, requires little inventory. A retail franchise, such as The Mole Hole, has to put inventory control and purchasing methodology on center stage. It is a major consideration in the success of a retail business. The wrong merchandise in the wrong quantities during the wrong season will spell disaster.

Now it's up to you. Evaluate you own franchise needs. Develop a plan. Incorporate the techniques of developing specifications, quantity analysis, bidding, storage, insurance, purchasing personnel training, and inventory control systems as they best fit your operation. Encourage the participation of your franchisor as well as your fellow franchisees.

ENDNOTES

[1] "Fortune Forecast/Testing Time For Lean Inventories," *Fortune*, August 10, 1992, p. 18.

[2] Carol Ellison, "Optimizing Network Resources, LAN Inventory Software," *PC*, June 30, 1992, p. 297.

CHAPTER 11

Crime as a Business Cost

In talking with franchisees and discussing their business costs, seldom is the cost of crime taken into consideration when the truth is that it *must*. In this chapter, we will discuss some of the crimes common to small businesses, and some of the actions that are necessary to deter these crimes. Prevention of crime and control of crime-related costs is a realistic objective.

Burglary

The crime of *burglary* is that of unlawful entry. The act of taking something, once they have entered the premises, is *robbery*. Let's first consider burglary.

There are certain situations that make burglary more likely. Burglars look for situations where they can enter quickly, make a minimum of noise (or less noise than will likely arouse attention) and where it is unlikely they will be seen by others. Recognizing this, you should structure the atmosphere of your business and the facility to make these situations as unlikely as possible.

After hours, leave the front and rear lights on around your building to discourage would-be burglars. Use bright lights, both inside and in the outside areas around your building. Some companies will install lights for the good of the entire neighborhood to protect their business. It is sometimes possible to get the city or the local utility company to install street lights in the vicinity of your business that will serve to protect your business along with others in the area. If appropriate for your type of business, erect sturdy fences around the property to discourage easy entry. In these cases, install lights at the gates. Use a watchdog if this is appropriate and possible.

On the entry doors to your building or store, install pry-proof frames. Since burglars often use crow bars, anything less will be easy prey. Secure all locks and doors. The use of cylinder-type locks is essential, so easy entry isn't obtained by picking the lock. Remember that one criterion used by burglars is a situation in which they can move quickly. Anything that will cause the burglar to take more time to enter the premises or make more noise will be a deterrent to the crime.

Whenever possible, use grates on exposed windows and all skylights. Skylights have been regularly used for entry and are especially vulnerable. Another less-known means of entry are the trapdoors in the ceilings of some buildings.

For example, a new business was set to open in a shopping center. On a Sunday morning, the company president went down to the office to check on some materials. He discovered that all the new furnishings and equipment had been stolen during the night. It was made to appear that the burglars had entered through a rear door. Police suspected the cleaning people had left the back door unlocked. However, the owners had known the staff of the janitorial company for over five years, and were absolutely convinced of their honesty. They decided to pursue other answers. The president later spotted a trapdoor on the roof. It had been installed by the builders of the shopping center. The person renting the facility could not spot the door from the inside, as there were ceiling tiles blocking the view. One would have to go to the roof generally to be in a position of seeing this door. No effort had been made to lock the trap door. Careful examination, following the discovery, showed that the burglars had entered the premises through the door on the roof and later carefully replaced the ceiling tiles. Had the door not been dis-covered, they were clearly in a position to reenter at a future date, and rob the premises again.

Further investigation disclosed that there had been break-ins and robberies at other stores in that same shopping center. All of the stores that had been burglarized also had trapdoors on the roof. The solution was initially easy. The trapdoors were sealed and locked. However, there were other issues. A key question was whether there had been inside help from personnel who managed the shopping center. Was it simply ignorance or lack of concern on their part? Were they incompetent? Whatever, the result was the same. A num-ber of businesses had been entered into and robbed. Not only was precious business time lost in answering police questions and filing for insurance, but additional business operational time was lost, as new furnishings and equipment had to be ordered and delivered in order to resume or start up the business operations.

A similar break-in occurred when air vents were removed from the roof of a supermarket. It was found that the burglars had entered the store through the opening after these air vents had been removed. The caution here is to check for such entry points into your business establishment, and then take immediate action to seal them.

Build In Burglarproofing from the Start

Alertness on the part of businesspersons before the start-up of opera-tions can pay off in great dividends later on. If you never have to face the problem of a break-in or robbery, you have saved not only money, but also significant trauma and fear on the part of employ-ees. By planning to structure the premises to make it burglarproof or a deterrent to burglars, you could save time and money you'll never have to calculate.

A minor research project—checking on the experiences neighbor-ing businesses have had in terms of crime—can cue you in on the potential problems in your locale. If the situation is severe, you may want to invest in a burglar alarm system. There are a large variety of systems. It pays to spend some time at police headquarters in your community and at several burglar alarm companies, getting an idea as to the necessity for investing in such a system, the comparative costs of varying systems, as well as their comparative benefits. Be sure the alarm company services their accounts 24 hours a day. A breakdown in the system should be serviced immediately.

As I've mentioned, break-ins are not only costly in lost equipment and lost business time, there is also a large emotional cost to be considered. Crowbars are used to break down doors, destroy desks, open files and safes. Often wanton destruction and vandalism accompanies burglaries. Broken glass, soiled furnishings, and personal items can cause emotional upheaval to someone who has taken pride in the neat, orderly, attractive business environment. Equipment and furnishings that gave you a sense of pride one day can cause a personal setback after there has been wholesale destruction of your premises.

Train Employees

It is important to implement a training program for your employees. Burglaries and robberies are a major business concern today. There are steps that you can take to better prepare your employees for such an occurrence. In this case an ounce of prevention can be worth a lot more than a pound of cure. You may save lives and prevent injuries. You may be able to cut financial losses substantially. The following are some guidelines for an employee training program. You could organize such a program in your franchisee advisory council with the support of your franchisor.

Burglar Alarms

Advice from a former burglar,[1] now safely in jail, is as follows:

Systems to Avoid:

1. *Door and window systems*—These are easily spotted by burglars and are avoided. They can then enter through roof vents or use jumper wires to deactivate the system.

2. *Electronic eye systems*—Once aware of such systems, the burglar can avoid them.

Effective Alarms:

1. *Proximity alarms*—These are activated by noise. They are sensitive to any noise that they are programmed to register.

Additional recommendations:

1. Be sure employees know how to use them.

2. Have them central-station wired. Most people today ignore the ring of alarms.

3. Seek professional assistance in the installation of an alarm system and in the training of your staff in the use of such systems and in the prevention of false alarms.

Locks:

1. Most experts agree that a pin-tumbler cylinder lock provides the most security.[2] Most have three to seven pins. Professionals agree that at least five pins are necessary in order to deter burglars.

2. Dead bolts should be used. Dead bolts cannot be opened by sliding a piece of flexible material between the door edge and the door jamb. This does not make them burglary-proof, however. One Weight Watchers franchisee learned that lesson when burglars tore out the door moldings to gain entrance using crow bars.

3. Use double-cylinder dead locks on glass doors. This means that a burglar cannot open the door without a key on both sides.

4. Use a knowledgeable locksmith to instruct staff on how to best protect themselves in using the locks and keys properly.

Keys:

1. Caution employees on the protection of keys.[3] Especially caution that they don't leave them with parking attendants. Unscrupulous individuals can duplicate keys and gain access to your facility.

2. Have a responsible employee in charge of key distribution. Have them take a periodic inventory. Be sure it is kept in a safe place.

3. If an employee leaves and doesn't return his key, re-key the store.

4. Don't master key; it weakens security.

5. Have one key for outer doors: another for inner doors.

6. Stamp "Do Not Duplicate" on keys. It's not foolproof, but it does help to hinder unauthorized copying.[4]

7. Don't carry a key chain that indicates the store's address.

Lights:

1. Use lighting generously inside and outside.[5]

2. You can put your lights on a timing system to go on at dusk and off at daylight. Be sure a responsible employee is in charge of adjusting the timing throughout the year, and turning them on and off, if necessary. Otherwise an automatic, photo-electric eye system may be installed.

3. Mercury and metallic lights are good for illuminating exterior walls.

4. Good inside lighting helps police on patrol. Again, someone must be trained to be responsible for turning on the system before closing.

Your Business Safe

Before investing in a safe,[6] do some investigating. There are some that are merely fire-resistant. This type safe is very important if you are storing business papers. There are others that are burglary-resistant as well as fire-resistant. They are designed to guard against ripping, punching, chopping, or burning. Safes can serve to protect your cash, checks, and important documents such as contracts and leases.

Placement of the safe is another issue. There are different schools of thought on this point. One simply is to keep it out of view, so no one is aware that there is a safe on the premises. The potential problem with this is that a burglar can be working on breaking into the safe in total privacy. The other school of thought, preferred by police, is that the safe should be placed out in the open, so that any policeman on patrol, or other passerby, can readily view anyone attempting to break into it. Whatever you decide to do, bolt the safe in place. Should you opt to install an alarm system, police experts recommend it be of the silent type wired to a central station.

There are some additional, generally accepted principles that you can readily implement to keep your valuables out of the hands of burglars. One is to keep the cash register empty and open after closing. This will prevent a burglar from prying open and damaging your cash register.

Keep minimum cash necessary in the safe, and be sure employees are aware that this is your policy. Make sure the safe is bolted down to the building structure.

Before closing make sure an employee:

1. Puts everything into the safe that should be there

2. Makes note of the serial numbers of high denomination bills

3. Checks to make sure the safe is properly locked

4. Activates the burglar alarm

General Tips for Employees

In the day-to-day operations of business, there are procedures that can diminish loss of inventory to "non-purchasing customers."[7]

1. When storing clothing on racks, alternate the direction of hangers to prevent burglars sweeping clothes off the racks.

2. Tie the cords of electrical appliances together.

3. Display expensive goods in the center of the store, but not all in the same place, making it more difficult for the burglar to make a quick sweep of items.

Armed Robbery

Armed robbery is a crime of violence, and must be recognized as such. The main thing is to remain calm. The experts urge you to avoid violence by not exciting the armed criminal. Here are some expert recommendations it would be wise to pass on to your staff beforehand.

1. Obey the instructions given by the robber.

2. Try to stay alert and remember as much as possible about the criminal. Notice any identifying marks. Analyze the robber's height, weight, skin, hair, and eye color.

3. If the robber has a getaway car, try to remember the model, the color, and the license plate whenever possible. Doing these things necessitates calm on your part.

4. Don't try to play the hero. The goal is to provide the police with as much information as possible so that your stolen property can be recovered and the criminals apprehended.

5. If there is a possibility of evidence such as fingerprints, be very careful not to touch or to destroy any of the evidence. Leave things as they were. Allow the police inspection team to do their job.

The following are some techniques you can use to train staff to better avoid robberies.[8] Instruct staff to:

1. Always open and close the premises in teams.

2. Move away from the cash register to a secluded area to count cash.

3. Observe and report (by pre-arranged signal) any suspicious persons who may be "casing" the premises.

4. Have an additional employee or guard accompany the carrier of cash, checks, and securities.

Credit Card Thefts

Credit card thefts are a growing problem. It takes a week before the list of stolen credit cards are sent to businesses. This delay causes some of the problems, since thieves often are aware of the period of time that they have to use these cards.

There are some training steps that you can use to have your staff better informed in how to avoid credit card fraud.

1. Check the expiration date to be sure card is current.

2. Be sure the name has not been altered on the card.

3. Be sure employees verify purchases and receive authorization above a certain dollar purchase amount.

4. If a customer's appearance is inconsistent with the type of purchase she is making, that should trigger suspicions. You can ask for additional ID. Also, you can check with your local police as to appropriate actions to take in this case. If you have an alert system to police headquarters or to a burglar alarm company, for instance, you may want to activate the alert.

5. If your clerk is suspicious as to whether the signature matches the card, always ask for additional identification. A procedure should be set up, within your company, so that police can be called in. No one likes to make waves, but there are often clear-cut examples where signatures did not match the cards and yet no attempt was made to identify the user of the cards. This encourages continued theft of credit cards, as the person using the card feels secure in being able to escape detection.

The important thing is that you have policies in place and that your employees know and understand these policies, and, most importantly, that they follow these policies and procedures. Scheduled, regular updates and reviews are in order.

Counterfeit Money

Most businesses escape attempts to use counterfeit money. There are frequently alerts in a community about the passing or attempted passing of fake currency. An excellent vehicle to spearhead such an alert would be the local Chamber of Commerce. The time to set up such a procedure would be before it is needed. Perhaps a task force could set up a training seminar for businesses and a follow-up procedure so, if it were needed, it could be put into practice immediately. If you have a large number of franchisees in an area, or if you're holding a regional seminar, the local police or private investigatory company could provide additional training for franchisees, managers, and staff. The local law enforcement agency would probably cooperate in such an effort, and federal authorities would support it.

Federal Reserve Notes, which are most readily available, have a green seal. These are available in denominations of $1, $2, $5, $10, $20, $50, and $100. U.S. Treasury notes have a red seal and are now only printed in $100 denominations. Treasury Certificates are no longer printed. When comparing bills, look for certain differences. Federal District Seal has a letter and number inside. J is the tenth letter of the alphabet, the J and 10 should correspond, or since B is second, the B and 2 should correspond. The letter and the number should always correspond. Serial numbers should match. Red and blue lines should be visible in the background. The squares in the background should not be filled in nor the lines broken. These and other details are clues to counterfeit bills. If a bill does not feel quite right, be suspicious. A person handling money becomes familiar with the feel.

Bad Checks

Personal checks[9] are another problem. Here are several things to watch for when accepting a personal check.

1. The company or bank name is rubber-stamped, the type face is irregular, or words are misspelled.

2. Poor spacing, blots, erasures, changes in ink color or thickness of lines indicate the check has been tampered with.

3. The date on the check is stale or post-dated.

4. The signature of the check is illegible.

5. The check has not been MICR-encoded.

6. The customer can't produce a photo ID with the check.

7. The address on the check and on the photo identification don't match.

8. The check edges have no perforations. One edge should be perforated from its removal from the check book. The only exception is government checks.

9. The check is in the low series (101-150)(101-150). This may signify a bad check because new checking accounts generally initiate checks with low numbers. This indicates that the account has not been established for very long.

10. There is writing interfering with the numbers at the bottom of the check. If someone writes checks and they don't have

money in the account yet, they could write their signature through numbers at the bottom of the check. This writing on the numbers interferes with the automatic sorting of the checks, and throws the check out. It will take a few additional days to clear.

11. The check is made out to two different people. (Bob Jones *or* Mary Smith, or Bob Jones *and* Mary Smith), or the amount is different in both places, or there are different inks.

12. The check is really a Xerox color copy. Wet fingers and see if the check smears.

Institute precautionary policies among your staff.

1. On travelers' checks, make the person sign their name in front of you. There are two numbers on the back of American Express checks. Check that these are the same. If one says $10, the other also should say $10.

2. Utilize a check guarantee insurance policy.

3. When taking identification for checks, a driver's license with a photo is best. Next best is another photo ID. You and your employees should be trained to check routinely the photo against the face of the person presenting the ID. However, one must be aware that there has been quite a racket in making forged driver's licenses. For example, a Colorado Driver's License does not tear because it has been laminated. You may legally use the tear test to see if the laminated driver's license will tear. You may check other states' drivers licenses for similar protection.

Fake Identification

Now that we've encouraged you to get proper identification from people, we suggest you teach your employees how to be better prepared to spot fake IDs.[10] There are some procedures in place to better help you in the detection process.

1. Repeat some information back to the party incorrectly. For example if the address is 1515 Elm Street, mention 1615 Elm

as their address. People with fake IDs may not have paid attention to details.

2. A typographical error is a clue.

3. Be suspicious if the name, city, and state of the issuing agency is typed in as opposed to being printed.

4. Look for raised edges around photographs. This could mean that a substitution was made.

5. Look for flaws in the lamination process. This could be a sign of tampering.

6. Check that the typing on various parts of the card match. A mismatch is a clue to a fake ID.

7. Check the signature of the holder to the signature on the card.

8. Be aware of excessive nervousness on the part of the party providing the ID. This could be a cue to a problem.

Shoplifting

Shoplifting is a crime that we hear a great deal about. It is a crime of grave national concern because the majority of shoplifters are under 30 years of age. In fact, teenagers are the major offenders. According to the SBA,[11] 50 percent of shoplifters are young-juvenile offenders. The average shoplifter has at least three items in their possession when leaving, making this a costly crime to business.

Shoplifters break out into two groups: the deliberate thieves, either professionals or amateurs who come to your store specifically to steal; or impulsive shoplifters, who are overcome by temptation. Professionals are highly skilled and difficult to spot. Amateurs steal for themselves or friends.[12]

The tough decision facing franchisees is often whether to prosecute the shoplifter. My recommendation is to do so. Evidence has shown that when there is no serious follow-up to a shoplifting, other teenagers will frequently seek out the same business as the target for future shoplifting. Failure to prosecute can be an invitation to increase the potential crime in your franchised business. There is also the question of social responsibility to other shopkeepers as well.

Alerting the family of the shoplifter that the individual is in need of help also can be beneficial to that individual. Since shoplifting is considered to be a relatively minor crime to everyone except the store owner, realistically, one can expect that the repentant shoplifter probably will get more help than punishment. In addition, most teenagers will never have the shoplifting information entered into their criminal records. On the other hand, success at minor crimes without punishment can encourage one to go on to bolder, more aggressive criminal activities.

Since such a large proportion of shoplifters are teenagers, it has been shown that this criminal activity in some areas centers around the 3–6 P.M. time period during the school year. The time period expands during the summer months. Alertness to these patterns can help you structure surveillance during peak problem hours.

There are some very definite steps you can take in training your employees in avoiding shoplifting.[13] Remember shoplifters are thieves. They cost your business and other businesses a lot of money each year.

1. Most shoppers are concerned with their own business. Shoplifters are the opposite, they are constantly on guard.

2. Shoplifters like to carry many bulky bags. This is their way to disguise what they have pilfered.

3. Watch out for people with loose, oversized clothing. This is a common way for professionals to hide merchandise that they have taken.

4. Shoplifters avoid crowded store hours, and can be found in less crowded or empty parts of a store.

5. They are aimless and tend to wander. Real buyers have a purpose for being in the store. They are looking for something in particular.

6. Professionals often use a diversion or distraction. An unusual event in the store can be a warning sign that a team is working. Some of the things to look for are:
   a. Employee's time being taken with pointless questions
   b. A seemingly faked argument
   c. A dropped or spilled rack of merchandise

d. A "phony" medical emergency

Steps to Avoid Shoplifting

Training employees is essential. All of the following items should be implemented and then employees trained in the effective use of these systems:[14]

1. Hang signs warning shoplifters that you will prosecute.

2. Plan to follow up on that threat.

3. Hang wide-area or convex mirrors strategically to avoid blind spots.

4. Display expensive merchandise in security cases.

5. Place potentially targeted items near check-out counters.

6. Block off unused check-out stands to avoid easy exit.

7. Be visible. Be available. If you see a suspicious party, ask if you can help him.

8. Consider using uniformed or plainclothed store detectives, if necessary. You must, of course, measure this cost against the degree of theft that you are experiencing.

9. Have cashiers and store personnel alert to switched tags on merchandise.

10. Lay out the store in such a way as to avoid shoplifting. This plan can be devised with your franchisor and fellow franchisees. Use employee imput.

11. A two-way mirror can possibly be installed and helpful in certain situations.

12. Use tamper-proof price tags.

13. Implement security hangers on expensive merchandise.

14. Utilize electronic article surveillance devices. These include door alarms to be activated if the shoplifter attempts to leave the premises with the items without having paid for them.[15]

Employee Theft

Another area of criminal activity that the franchisee has to consider is internal theft. That is, when your own employees are stealing from you. If profit and production appear to be down, you may be experiencing employee theft. There are a variety of patterns to internal theft. Sometimes an employee pockets a cash payment. Perhaps she sells an item to a friend at a discounted price. Failure to give a customer a sales receipt and then pocketing the cash becomes a temptation.

Kim Carl, a Pak Mail franchisee in North Charleston, South Carolina, suspected employee theft of postage stamps. She became proactive and instituted inventory procedures to curb this internal crime. She also encourages you to implement theft protection systems, even if not 100 percent foolproof. If employees know that theft-prevention systems are in place, and that you are aware of the temptation and are aggressively working to prevent it, they will be less likely to risk being caught.

Ms. Carl also has a negative incentive she wants to share with her fellow franchisees. At one time she initiated a program to reward staff for having their books balanced at the end of the day. She also came to realize that there are occasional discrepancies in a cash business. What she soon discovered was that this in fact gave employees an incentive to steal overages, thereby balancing accounts at the end of the day. She was actually tempting her own employees to steal; not her initial intent at all. She quickly changed that particular incentive program. The message here is to think through any changes you plan to implement. Always ask yourself the question: what can result from these changes?

You also may take the initiative and talk with those employees you trust and with whom you feel you are on excellent terms, drawing out their suggestions for plugging security gaps and preventing future thefts. Even employees who are supportive but unwilling to report on other employees whom they know or believe to be stealing will perhaps clue you in on the procedures to prevent such future thefts. You may even find yourself approaching a trusted employee who may be stealing. This conversation alone may be a sufficient alert to stop such activities immediately. The employee now knows that you are aware of such activities and will take the necessary steps to prevent them.

Useful suggestions can come from employees who are honest and feel a responsibility to management. These suggestions should be implemented whenever possible. Just listening, and not attempting to follow through, may discourage employees from assisting management in the future.

White Collar Crime

Employee theft is included in what is considered to be white collar crime. White collar crimes are those crimes perpetrated by office workers and without violence. The following excerpt is from *Management Accounting* magazine:

> White collar theft is a problem that is increasing. It is particularly prevalent in decentralized, impersonal companies. It can be controlled by careful screening of applicants in sensitive positions. It also helps to inform employees of company policy relating to internal theft. A well-defined policy of internal security should be developed. One study showed that there were clearly two types of white collar criminals. One you would readily suspect, the individual with a history of extensive criminal activity. The other, the real problem to management, is the person who appears to be healthy and stable and who has no criminal history. Economic bravado to outwit the system breed temptation and opportunity which can all be motivators in the white collar criminal.[16]

There are some clues to employee theft. Here are some of the steps that you can implement in your business in order to better protect yourself:[17]

1. Tighten observation of employees. Unusual behavior or being in areas they do not belong can be a clue.

2. Key workers who have responsibilities for handling money should be screened. Break out responsibilities for money and record-keeping among two or more employees.

3. Be careful when giving long-term and highly trusted employees total responsibilities in areas that can cause temptation. The tendency is to remove systematic checking systems from

these employee's jobs simply because they are fully trusted. These are the very employees that are then thrust into a tempting position to embezzle and steal. Do periodic screening of all employees, including those in whom you have full trust.

4. Check into employees who appear to be living beyond their means. Be suspicious.

5. Be aware that people who are chronic complainers often feel unappreciated and are subject to criminal behavior.

6. Watch employees who are subject to substance abuse. They may need funds to support their habits.

7. Employees with specific problems like gambling should be a source of concern. They may become desperate.

8. Cash register information to check on:

   a. gaps in transaction numbers

   b. too many "no sale" transactions

   c. an unusually large number of over-rings and voids

   d. a pattern of consistent small overages. This could mean that the cashier has been under-reporting small amounts and leaving excess overages to accumulate.

Embezzlement

Perhaps the cruelest form of employee crime is embezzlement. A very trusted individual in a very trusted position in your firm sets up a pattern of theft that generally goes undetected for a long period of time. It has happened to governments, to churches, to businesses, and yes, to franchisees. The person usually appears motivated and efficient. He handles multiple tasks, and you, as the franchisee, tend to welcome that added help from a competent person. You turn more and more responsibility over to him with fewer and fewer checks on what he is doing.

Ask yourself these questions.[18] If the answers are yes, you are vulnerable:

1. Is the person who handles your cash also responsible for recording the cash?

2. Is the person who pays for or orders inventory also the one who receives the materials?

3. Are two or fewer people responsible for the accounting functions?

4. Is only one person responsible for reviewing financial statements?

5. Is your review of financial journals sporadic?

If you find you are vulnerable, change the above procedures immediately. In addition:

1. Reconcile bank statements once a month, no ifs, ands, or buts.

2. Review canceled checks and endorsements on a monthly basis.

3. Compare payroll checks with your current employee list.

4. Question funds transferred between bank accounts.

5. Track the number of credit card bills you sign each month.

6. Make sure someone is responsible for reviewing the reconciliations each month. Then, verify the reconciliations.

7. Never sign blank checks.

8. Don't use rubber stamp signatures for checks.

Check if your employees are overly possessive about their work. The Comptroller of the Currency and most state bank regulatory agencies require that bankers take two full weeks off, away from their job, to be sure that others step in to do the work. It's an excellent check-and-balance system in place. Yes, it's extra work when you feel you're overworked already. Nevertheless, if you do not put these systems in place, you may be sowing the seeds of the destruction of your franchised business. The results of embezzlement can and have been catastrophic. Don't let it happen to you. It is preventable.

The Bureau of National Affairs in 1988 claimed that U.S. businesses lose some $15 to $25 million annually to dishonest employees. This shocking statistic has not improved in recent years. In fact, some private investigation firms now specialize in detecting employee theft.

Illegal Rebates

Another form of employee theft is the taking of illegal rebates, sometimes colloquially called "kickbacks," from vendors. If you suspect that this is taking place, and you are concerned that you are in fact subsidizing your personnel in the purchasing department, a shakeup of staff may be necessary. Having proof is essential. You may have to hire a private investigator. You may even have to get involved in purchasing procedures yourself for a sufficient period of time to uncover such activities. If employees are taking rebates from vendors, be assured, you are paying for them.

Riots and Other Man-Made Disasters

On April 29, 1992, a riot broke out in Los Angeles. It was the immediate result of the acquittal of four policeman accused of beating Rodney King. There has been a recent history of riots: the Watts riots in Los Angeles in 1965, as well as other riots in Detroit, Miami, and New York City. Many businesses were damaged; 5,200 shops, markets, and buildings were burned. Initial estimates were of a billion dollars in damage. Some believe the estimates are too low.[19] One British magazine surmised that the loss of 200,000 jobs in Los Angeles along with the influx of migrants was a cause. It also noted that no shops were damaged on famed Rodeo Drive.[20]

Planning to avoid such horrendous man-made disasters takes a different form. If you are operating a business in this climate, you will have to get involved and link up with other franchisees and community merchants in the formation of community economic development task forces for strategic, community-wide planning. Together, you need to address the identification of root problems and come up with programs to eliminate them. Draw from among yourselves committed, competent leaders and the capital to execute your resulting plan.

Crime from Manhattan to Smalltown, USA

You may immediately assume that crime is highest in the big cities. In reality, statistics vary. New York City, which is considered to be synonymous with crime in some circles, is actually safer than many other cities. However, the density of the population, the visibility of the crimes, the newspapers and television stations that focus in on such situations, make the city appear more dangerous than it actually is. On a per capita basis, the crime rate in a small community can equal that of major cities. How does that affect you as a franchisee?

You have to know your city, your town. The size will make a difference in the crimes that you may experience. In a smaller community, you are more likely to know who belongs and who does not. Strangers are more visible, more recognizable. They also are easier to track down. In a larger city, criminals can literally get lost in a crowd. Franchises located in transient areas are particularly vulnerable to crime because of a lack of stability and identification in the community.

So in large cities and small, franchisees must recognize that crime is an economic cost of their business. It must be figured into the business plan. Prevention of crime is a cost, too. Executive time must be allocated periodically to be sure that the most advanced and best crime prevention techniques your business can realistically afford have been implemented. The goal clearly is to prevent the greater loss or wanton destruction of property and merchandise, as well as the loss of furniture, business supplies and equipment, displays, and production tools. In addition, and most importantly, you want to provide the most safe and secure environment for your employees that you can.

ENDNOTES

[1] "How To Do Everything Right," *Bottom Line Personal*, Boardroom Reports, New York, NY, 1992.

[2] *Preventing Burglary and Robbery Loss*, Small Business Administration, Small Marketers Aid No. 134, Washington DC, 1975.

[3] Ibid.

[4] "How To Do Everything Right," *Bottom Line Personal*, Boardroom Reports, New York, NY, 1992.

[5] *Preventing Burglary and Robbery Loss.*

[6] Ibid.

[7] "Money Wise," *The Denver Post*, Denver, CO, December 8, 1991.

[8] "Protecting Your Business From Embezzlement, Burglary, and Robbery," Fireman's Fund American Insurance Co., not dated.

[9] "Crime Prevention for Small Business," *Small Business Reporter*, Bank of America, San Francisco, CA, 1982.

[10] "How To Do Everything Right," *Bottom Line Personal*, Boardroom Reports, New York, NY, 1992.

[11] Joe Dacy II, "They Come To Steal, How To Prevent Shoplifting at Your Small Business," IB/September–October 1991.

[12] Ibid.

[13] Ibid.

[14] Ibid.

[15] "Crime Prevention for Small Business."

[16] *Accounting*, 1980.

[17] "Crime Prevention for Small Business."

[18] Dorothy Simonelli, "To Catch A Thief, A Small Business Owner's Guide To Preventing Embezzlement," IB/September–October 1992.

[19] "Can L.A. Rise From the Ashes?," *Business Week*, May 18, 1992, pp. 42–44.

[20] "26 Scenes from A Riot," *The Economist*, May 9–15, 1992.

CHAPTER 12

The Ravages of Nature on Business

We all are familiar with the plight of farmers in the 1930s when a drought hit plains states like Oklahoma and Kansas. Due to inadequate water, incorrect methods of plowing the soil, and strong winds, many farmers were faced with the total destruction of their crops and their dreams. To make matters worse, top soil eroded and blew away, making future farming on the land difficult, if not impossible, for many years to come.

Businesses as well as farms can and have been wiped out from natural disasters. Some businesspeople have the foresight to plan for the potential problems caused by nature, because they recognize that natural disasters can temporarily derail or even ruin their businesses.

Almost all areas in the United States hold the potential for natural disasters. Unfortunately, there are plenty of business and industrial parks in flood plains and in earthquake-prone areas along major faults. There are other business areas subject to hurricanes, tornadoes, and volcanoes. It seems fashionable to take a fatalistic point of view and say, "What will happen, will happen," but this should *not* be your point of view. You can take precautions against the ravages of nature as another business responsibility to be dealt with. This chapter will show that your franchised business can be directly or indirectly impacted by the vagaries of nature, and suggest some precautions to take to help increase your chances of coming through a disaster with minimal or no damage.

First, find out how prone your business might be to a natural disaster. Then be the judge of how much precaution to take. When doing site selection with your franchisor, be sure to discuss this aspect of site selection. If your business is located in Miami, you could have considered yourself warned; since 1987, weather experts have said a big hurricane was going to be coming. In 1992 it came in the form of mega-storm Hurricane Andrew. Or you could expect a semi-arid region like Colorado to experience another drought. If you live and work in the Texas panhandle, tornadoes are potential hazards.

Here are some examples of how unselective and unforgiving nature can be—taking homes, businesses, and, in some cases, lives.

Flooding

On September 11, 1977, the weather forecasters in Topeka, Kansas, predicted a 70 percent chance of thunderstorms for that night and/or the following day. A thunderstorm started shortly after midnight on the 12th of September. Six inches of rain fell that night, saturating the local drain basin. Meanwhile, Kansas City was sunny and unaffected. On the 12th, forecasters in spite of the sunshine were predicting the possibility of severe thunderstorms late in the day. At 5:45 P.M. flash flood warnings were sounded. At around eight that evening, rain started falling in Kansas City, so heavily the major league baseball game was canceled. People filed out to return home, many driving to their deaths. Brush Creek had risen to 22 feet and sent a wall of water into the Country Club Plaza. In spite of warnings, local residents were complacent and went on about their lives. Water poured into restaurants, stores. At its greatest flow, it achieved 261,800 gallons of water per second. This indeed had catastrophic results. The velocity of Brush Creek was about 20 feet a second, or about seven times more than it takes to knock a person off their feet. It was also enough of a force to overturn autos.[1]

Businesses of every type were damaged in the mall. People knew of the vulnerability, but the Country Club Plaza was and is the place to open an upscale business in Kansas City. Businesses that choose to locate in this mall must do so with their eyes open and all precautions in place.[2]

Even floods that primarily affect farm areas, like the September 15, 1992, flooding in Iowa, caused by 12-16 inches of rainfall, cause disruption. Roads turn into lakes and lakes become rivers. Bridges wash out. The economy of the entire community is affected.

Those floods that hit towns and cities are even more devastating. On April 13, 1979, 20 inches of rain fell, causing the Pearl River in Mississippi to rise 25 feet above flood level. Jackson, Mississippi, felt the disastrous consequences of this overflowing river, even though it did not rain in Jackson itself.

Citizens of the city, prisoners from the local prison, and National Guardsmen tried to hold back the tide, but to no avail. Most of the buildings in the thriving Lakeland Drive business district were swamped with water. The decision was made by city officials that the situation was so grave, and the magnitude of the emergency so large, that they could only concentrate on saving lives and not public property. This included businesses, and of course franchised businesses. The officials simply could not protect the property of individuals and businesses, and businesses were hit hard by the flooding. For the next five days, example after example of the plight of the business community were recorded.

The B-Line Gas Station and Convenience Store was filled with four feet of water, and about $12,000 in merchandise was ruined. Kemper Insurance Company had to move its files to dry ground, so business could go on as usual after the flood. At the Coliseum Ramada Inn, 300 guests were evacuated and the motel closed. The whole first floor of a new wing was flooded, and the carpeting on the second floor of the wing was ruined. In all, 730 businesses were flooded, $168 million dollars (1979 dollars) were lost in homes, businesses, and personal property in five days. At the peak of the crisis, 18,500 telephones were out. Businesses were shut down, and three electrical stations were out of commission.

A follow-up to the Jackson flood a year later showed lingering effects of the flood on the local business community. At least one new business that expected to locate in Jackson and employ 400 persons decided against it. They chose a site in another state. Other businesses avoided locating their businesses in the Greater Jackson Industrial Park, which is partly located in the flood plain. In fact, even though large portions of the city were not hit by the flood and some businesses in the Industrial Park were not affected, many businesses have refused to locate either in the Industrial Park or anywhere else in Jackson. However costly the lesson, it now is known exactly which areas in Jackson are affected by flooding and which are not so safe and appropriate site selection can be made.

Steps you can take to avoid flood damage:

1. Check the local zoning before buying property or signing a lease to assure that you are not in a flood zone.

2. Check to see if you're in the path of an old dam.

3. Build up one or two steps, if you can.

4. Have an inventory storage or evacuation plan in place. Be sure that all staff members understand the evacuation plan and all emergency procedures. Invest in the necessary equipment to carry out the plan, i.e., a forklift.

5. Keep all records in duplicate and stored in a safe place. This often means off-site. In today's age of computers, that shouldn't be difficult. Back up your files weekly or monthly, and move the disk to another safe spot. It could be a fire-proof vault in your home or a bank vault. Make sure your insurance records are among these stored and protected records.

6. Make sure accurate, up-to-date inventory files are safely stored. In case of mass destruction, it will help you quickly prove your claim. Be sure you can authenticate the value of these items. That means purchasing and, if appropriate, manufacturing records be included.

7. Check on the availability of flood insurance if you are vulnerable to this kind of natural disaster.

8. Perhaps most important, pay attention to the weather adviseries, and take them seriously.

Drought

Water—either too much or too little—can be a major environmental consideration for many businesses. Floods, such as the one in Jackson, Mississippi, can cause severe, unexpected damage in a very short time. Droughts also can cause economic losses over a longer period of time. North Dakota farmers, who produced 252 million bushels of wheat in 1979, struggled in the next year through the driest spring in 44 years. In the very best areas of the state, rainfall averaged less than three inches for the year. Farmers who seeded wheat in the late spring in the southwestern part of the state found only a dry dirt crust. One farmer was forced to sell 45 head of cattle because he had no feed for them. On land that brought 30 bushels of wheat an acre in 1979, farmers were lucky to yield 15 bushels in 1980. Again in 1988, large parts of the U.S. experienced unusually high temperatures accompanied by a lack of rain. In the rich Midwest farm belt, crops dried up, topsoil blew away, and cattle were sent to market early. This has happened before and it will happen again. Franchise businesses operate in farm communities, too. There are the familiar franchised restaurant chains, along with Ben Franklin stores, Ace Hardware, Computerland, General Nutrition Centers, PIP Printing, Decorator Den, Athlete's Foot, and more. When farm income is affected, these businesses also are affected. If you have a franchise in a farm-based community, you have to consider this weather phenomenon in your long-term planning.

The businesses in these areas affected by the accompanying 100-degree heat for long periods of time were additionally impacted by high energy costs. Air conditioning bills mounted. Business owners in these areas had extremely high utility bills during the period. Midwest businesses were affected additionally by the accompanying situation when the Mississippi River dropped to unprecedented levels. Barges and other river vehicles couldn't navigate. As a direct result, delivery costs on many items escalated. The U.S. Army Corps of Engineers stepped in at federal government direction to help, but their ability was limited. This was an unpredictable cost as a result of a form of drought.

The effect of drought was different in Colorado in 1976 and 1977 than in North Dakota. Colorado farmers were better prepared to handle these problems. Many had irrigation of one form or another.

However, the drought caused havoc on Colorado's western slope (the name popularly given to the mountain communities in the central and western part of the state). Communities like Aspen, Vail, Steamboat Springs, and Breckenridge, which have gained world fame for their ski and shopping facilities, faced a winter with little or no snow. Some of the ski areas were fortunate enough to have expensive snow-making equipment. However, the equipment only served to keep minor ski slopes available to skiers. The major part of the mountains were not serviced with snow-making equipment. This problem did not simply affect ski slopes and skiers from around the world who vacation in Colorado. It had a domino effect and affected such businesses as airlines, limousine services, buses, car rentals, hotels, motels, restaurants, sporting goods stores, local food markets, banks, and on and on. The empty ski slopes meant empty condominiums and hotel rooms. Empty rooms in turn meant empty restaurants and stores. Real estate developers, who had speculated and built condominium units for sale, found themselves with unsalable units and faced foreclosures from banks.

What does this mean to franchisees? Think of the franchised businesses that fill the above categories. We're talking about Re/Max, Century 21, Holiday Inn, Ramada Inn, Village Inn Pancake House, Pizza Hut, McDonald's, Midas Muffler, Hertz Car Rental, Service Master, Radio Shack, Mole Hole and more. Laborers suffered, too. Many workers had moved to these ski areas because of their usually dependable employment picture. Among them were construction laborers, waitresses, clerical help, maids, housemen, waiters, busboys, dishwashers, and ski instructors. When business was down and the skiing wasn't available, many people left these towns. Businesses had a shortfall of qualified personnel in some cases. Retail businesses found themselves unable to reach a break-even point, and owners were forced to close or sell out to those with the financial ability to carry them through hard times.

When the ski resorts of New England were similarly hurt by a lack of snow in the winter of 1979-1980, because of the earlier experience of the Colorado drought, they found Small Business Administration Emergency Disaster Loans available to them.

There has been some criticism of aid going to ski resort areas, that this was governmental aid going to the wealthy. However, examination of the facts demonstrates that the small businesses in these areas clearly met the definition of small businesses damaged by the ravages of nature, and they were entitled to the aid. Many were family-owned-and-operated franchised businesses.

Steps to take to avoid drought damage:

1. If you have landscaping, use xeriscaping, which is landscaping that requires little or no additional water.

2. Install water-saving equipment whenever possible. In parts of California, the long drought of the 1980s and early 1990s has resulted in very high water usage fees, along with severe restrictions.

3. If your business is heavily dependent on abundant water, take this into consideration when locating. There are variances even within a metropolitan area. Different municipalities may have different sources of water.

4. Check the latest technology. Colorado ski areas have invested heavily for the past 10 years in snow-making equipment. This is a long-term, capital investment demanding group cooperation. The result not only offsets the risk to nature, but actually prolongs the ski season by one to two months. This has smoothed out the cycles and lengthened the business season.

5. Work with your local Chamber of Commerce or community economic development organization to check into the long-range development of alternative sources of water. This has to be done long in advance. When the drought is here, little can be done short-term.

Resources, Energy Use, and Conservation

All this points out another business concern. An efficient energy system for your business now has to be looked at as an investment. As a franchisee, you need to conduct an energy analysis. Frequently, you can get help from your local public company energy provider, which will conduct such surveys at low or no cost to local customers. Short- and long-run costs should be evaluated. Energy leakage and waste should be stopped.

Some states make conservation even more financially appealing with energy tax incentives. These energy-saving measures can mean immediate savings on utility bills, along with tax benefits, investment tax credits, energy tax credits, depreciation, and, possibly, improved productivity.

Get help in conserving energy from your employees, too. Offer incentives for ideas and for implementation. You will increase their morale and improve respect for your management.

This is also a terrific opportunity for a committee of your franchise association, in cooperation with your franchisor, to develop a specific strategic plan designed to maximize employee involvement in energy efficiency and cost savings.

The following are some recommendations to help you in your energy and conservation planning:

1. Check the R-factors for insulation. Basically the R-factor is a measurement of how well a particular insulation resists the flow of heat. The higher the number, the more heat your business would hold on to.

2. If you lease or own a free-standing building, check for insulation around doors, windows, where brick and siding meet, and generally wherever building materials meet. Leaks can often be corrected by caulking or added weather-stripping.

3. If you have a business with direct outdoor access, building a two-door entrance prevents much of the heat of summer and the cold of winter from entering directly into your unit.

4. If the furnace is your responsibility, consider investment in a high-efficiency furnace. The payback for a $300 cost differential for a high-efficiency appliance is estimated to be three years.

5. Avoid waste. Turn off unused equipment, appliances, lights.

6. If you control the heating cycle, put in timed thermostats. Set the heat to go up to comfortable temperatures a half-hour before opening shop, and go down a half-hour before closing.[3]

Wind Damage

In June of 1990, winds ruined the framework of a new, 10,000-square-foot central production and office facility in Peoria, Illinois. The structure was designed to service PIP Printing stores in the area.

(PIP Printing is the nation's largest printing franchisor.) Winds, too, can have a devastating impact of your business, especially during construction phases.

Windstorms are considered dangerous when wind gusts reach 40 or more miles per hour. Hurricanes and typhoons are windstorms with winds moving at 73 or more miles per hour. Tornadoes are defined as violent, whirling winds.

Everyone had known for a long time that Miami was in the possible path of a killer hurricane. A weather meteorologist, Bryan Norcross, joined Miami's WTVJ, an NBC affiliate, in 1987. As weather specialist, he set about planning for the possible "Big One." When, in August of 1992, nature was unkind, Bryan was ready. For 22 consecutive hours, he was the voice of calm and preparation on radio and TV in Miami. He is directly credited for saving lives and preventing injuries. Some called the low death toll luck, but many directly attributed it to Bryan Norcross's knowledge, cool head, and in-depth planning for just such an inevitable happening.[4]

When the major hurricane, dubbed Andrew, struck south of Miami in the Homestead area, it created what is considered the largest natural disaster to ever hit the United States. It certainly was in dollar power. It is estimated that the damage to this area and then to the Louisiana coast after the hurricane regrouped and hit there, was to come to more than $30 billion.

Those of us that were not directly impacted watched the suffering and devastation. Whole neighborhoods were destroyed. Businesses gone. Banks closed. Roads blocked. Every business in this area was impacted directly or indirectly. In fact many businesses nowhere in the vicinity of Florida or Louisiana were to feel the backlash of Hurricane Andrew. Within days of the hurricane, the weekly Random Lengths Composite Index soared to $345 per 1,000 feet on August 28, compared with $298 the week before. Oriented strand board, a plywood substitute known as OSB, rose from $241 to $270, an increase of 25 percent.[5] Adverse weather in one part of the country or the world can influence your business costs, too, even though your business may be located in an area that was unaffected. If you were expanding your business in Seattle and needed these products, you would have felt the economic wrath of Hurricane Andrew.

Hurricanes have slammed into coastal cities in other years. Businesses and residences have experienced flooding, destruction, and, more recently, looting. Some businesses have been forced to remain closed for prolonged periods of repair and re-stocking of inventory. Loans have to be negotiated. Insurance claims must be made. Meanwhile, there is no income. Along with the financial cost, there is clearly an emotional cost to the owner.

Myrtle Beach, South Carolina-based PIP Printing franchisee, John Riley faced Hurricane Hugo in October 1990. Although his business was left untouched by the storm, debris from a destroyed fishing pier and four feet of water and mud were under his house when he returned home. Many other businesses were not so fortunate. In fact, he discovered that printing became a lifeline of sorts for the community. He was swamped with letters from management companies who needed to make claims on damaged buildings. Business from the natural disaster benefitted PIP Printing, ironically causing an increase in business while neighboring businesses suffered at the whims of nature.

Steps to take to avoid wind damage:

1. Keep portable, transistor radios on hand so you can get up-to-date emergency information.

2. Keep a cellular phone on hand in order to have open communication.

3. Carefully check or have checked that the building you're in meets or exceeds the local building and zoning codes.

4. If you are building in accordance with franchisor specifications, be sure that they take into account local risk factors.

5. Be sure old trees in the area are taken care of and regularly trimmed.

6. Be sure that signs are properly secured to avoid unnecessary blowing hazards.

7. Check that there are emergency procedures in place for your staff, and that they are familiar with these procedures.

8. Check that there are emergency procedures in place for your community. If not, get involved and help *get* them in place.

Earthquakes

Interestingly, even though there is a lot of information on earthquakes, research is not available readily on the dollar impact on businesses following an earthquake. Those who document such tragedies focus on the human suffering and the problems of individuals. The best advice would be to develop a plan of action if you are in an earthquake-prone area. If there is a group of like franchisees from your organization, develop the plan together. Be there to help one another. *Fortune* magazine profiled Safeway's management in the Bay area after the earthquake of October 17, 1989. Safeway had 240 stores in Northern California. One hundred forty suffered damage; 30 had to close. Because they had a plan of action, though, they were up and operating in all stores in a short time.[6]

Earthquake preparedness steps to take:

1. As with winds, keep transistor radios and cellular phones on hand.

2. Use architecturally approved earthquake plans. Some cities outside of California are earthquake-prone, and yet have no architectural guidelines. Get the most current information regarding earthquake building recommendations and use them.

3. Use shatter-proof glass.

4. Avoid locating in vulnerable areas. Most are diagramed.

5. If appropriate, carry earthquake insurance.

Volcanoes

Mount St. Helens, a volcano in Washington, erupted on May 18, 1980. The blast and subsequent eruptions wreaked havoc on the economic communities of Portland (Oregon), Seattle, and Spokane. Millions of tourist dollars were lost to those communities that summer. Conventions were canceled; tourists stayed home; and hotels, restaurants, and small retail businesses suffered severe losses. In spite of the fact that these communities are not that close to the volcano and their accumulation of volcanic ash was not great, television interviews of people wearing masks and cleaning ash off their cars were enough to convince many tourists to play it safe and not visit the Northwest that summer.

The eruption of Mount St. Helens was a somewhat predictable event, since it was considered to be an active volcano. However, it had not had a period of major activity since 1847. In terms of such events as volcanoes, that is a short period of time. Predictions are that this volcano can remain active over the next 20 or more years.

Only those living in the Pacific Northwest need be concerned about volcanos. The only states with potential vulnerability are California, Oregon, Washington, and Alaska. The volcanoes with the greatest potential for activity, along with Mount St. Helens, are considered to be Mount Baker in Washington and Mt. Lassen in Northern California. The cities of Seattle and Portland are considered to be subject to deluges of volcanic ash and services disruption as a result.[7] Volcanoes can have far greater impacts than hurting tourism. They can block sunlight and bring about global cooling. If you are in these areas, you may have to take precautions.[8]

Volcano protection steps

1. As in winds and earthquakes, keep transistor radios and cellular phones.

2. Take warnings seriously.

3. Check to see if there is insurance available.

4. Make sure your staff has a plan, is familiar with escape routes, and will act prudently.

Snowstorms

Businesses are affected by nature, whether there is a large-scale disaster or not. One evening during a snowstorm in Denver, three small business owners were comparing their problems. One, the owner of seven Burger King franchises, observed that he might as well close up that night, since very few people come out to eat on a night like that. Another business owner, the area Weight Watchers franchisee, indicated the same about her business. On a bad night like this, most of the Weight Watchers clients were likely to stay comfortably warm in their homes. The third business owner indicated that, for him, the day of the snowstorm was merely the latest in a long series of bad days. His construction business had been slow all winter long due to severe cold and continuing snow. His crews were at a standstill on three major projects. At the same time, due to the same snowstorm, owners of small service stations reported sharp increases in business. This was because of the many motorists who required special assistance during adverse driving conditions.

Not an emergency. Not a catastrophe. But an ordinary snowstorm can have a significant effect on your business. It can lead to a short-term or a long-term slump, or to a powerful increase in business activity, depending on the nature of the business itself. Knowing this, you can plan ahead.

The best step to protection is a plan. In Weight Watchers we had such a plan. Designated employees had the phone numbers of specific radio or television stations, plus a list of all staff persons working on a particular day or night. The staff member making the decision as to whether Weight Watchers classes would be canceled had the phone numbers of the calling team. When the decision was made that driving was too hazardous, the decision maker activated the team. All media was contacted as well as staff members. The staff stayed home. The membership knew to tune in to local stations giving weather-related closing announcements, and the emergency was handled in a routine manner. This kind of procedure had the added benefit of improving staff confidence in management and increased client good will. We were saying that we cared. Can such a plan be implemented in your business? Of course it can! And the time to do it is before the first snows fly or the first winds blow.

Fooling Nature

Find out if there is commercial insurance coverage available. There are professional office packages written with "all risk" coverage. This means that all risks are covered unless they are specifically exempted. Often earthquakes and land failure (mud slides and potholes) are excluded. If you are in an area prone to earthquakes and mud slides such as Southern California, along the San Andreas fault, it is necessary to check further to see if such protection can be written in an additional policy. "All risk" coverage spreads the risk for the insurance company, and therefore is reasonably priced.

If there is not a commercial policy available to cover your risk, check to see if there is government insurance available. This is sometimes the case. The government has taken an active interest in several problem areas where they have undertaken to make such insurance available. There is, for instance, a National Flood Insurance Program.

There is also business interruption insurance. That means if your business is shut down for a variety of acceptable reasons, you will be covered. The causes differ, so you will have to confer with your insurance agent. One word of caution regarding this type of insurance from an insurance specialist: Be sure to select an actual loss policy, not one for just six months or one year's benefits. This will better serve you in an emergency. Business interruption insurance could be a "lifesaver" in an emergency.

Taking the time and making the effort to check into appropriate insurance coverage can save much heartbreak afterward, when a disaster has already occurred. Many people have seen their franchised businesses go under because they have not planned ahead for the ravages of nature. Many such businesses are "extensions" of the individual, personally and economically. This means that a business disaster is, in reality, a personal disaster. If there is a potential hazard, know the risks that you are taking, evaluate the kinds of coverage available, and make the most appropriate decision regarding coverage.

Check into the city and/or county plans for such emergencies or disaster preparedness. As a community-minded citizen, you might take the initiative to start a project that could protect your city or town from a potential disaster, or to ensure the right kind of equipment is available should such a disaster occur. A well-thought-out plan of action might be enough to save lives and personal property, and avoid a community-wide disaster.

Sometimes it is possible to anticipate either slow days, or days that you might just close up shop because of the weather. When that is the case, maybe some of your business costs could be effectively reduced by planning ahead. If your business is closed because of a blizzard, for instance, will you pay your personnel? Will they be required to make up the time? You might decide that, to promote goodwill, you will pay your staff. But you might consider asking them to make up the missed hours. How can you accomplish this? If they are non-union employees, you may ask them to work extra hours or on a weekend. Or, you may want to ask them to work half-time or three-quarters time for the hours missed.

Whatever your solution, it is best to come up with it prior to the actual emergency situation. Staff morale should be a priority in these situations as with other items. Unpleasant surprises generally are not effective management tools regardless of the situations.

Should you be governed by a union agreement, you will have to follow the agreement to the letter when it comes to closing for various reasons. However, if there is a cooperative atmosphere, it may be well to ask for flexibility under especially adverse circumstances. It does not serve the union well to have the entire business's survival threatened.

Generally, the best time to come to such an agreement would be the same for union and non-union—that is, before it happens. Discuss hypothetical situations and how they could be handled best for the benefit of employer and employee.

Planning

Some general insurance tips from State Farm insurance agent, John W. Pifer of Englewood, Colorado:

1. Have 100 percent coverage or insurance to value endorsements for good, solid coverage.

2. Have full replacement cost on contents.

3. Choose a large, solid, reputable company that writes a substantial amount of business insurance.

4. Have an annual review of your insurance with your agent. You are entitled to good insurance counseling on a regular basis.

5. Keep complete financial records of inventory, fixtures, signs, and income. Keep copies of invoices, accounts receivable, accounts payable, and income projections, and keep them in a safe place, off-site. Insurance companies require these records in order to fully compensate you in an emergency.

6. Good documentation is essential. Take pictures, keep receipts. If you can, go through the premises periodically and videotape

everything. A videotape is an inexpensive way to keep an up-to-date record of inventory, displays, signs, etc.

7. The best way to buy insurance would be to buy comprehensive coverage that would include "all risk" protection. This would include settling, landslide, sewage backup, war, radiation, and smog. Special add-ons are available for flood and earthquake. These should be added when appropriate.

8. Don't cut back on insurance coverage. If the cost is too high, increase the deductible. With a higher deductible, the cost of the policy is reduced. Small claims are eliminated, but you are covered in a major incident.

These examples of environmental disasters and events are not meant to frighten you from opening or expanding your franchised business. However, they do show clearly that there are events that could radically change the economic picture for your business. We also have shown that you are not powerless. You can have plans in advance of environmental hazards or potential disasters. Lack of plans can be as dangerous to your business as inadequate capitalization and poor management. There are steps that can be taken to substantially reduce losses in a disaster, to statistically increase the potential for economic survival during the times that nature vents on you, yet recognize that the problem cannot be totally eliminated.

Finally, in a world where business often alienates us from the fragile nature of our lives, the communal spirit among franchisees becomes a refreshing change. For example, the case of Handle With Care Packaging Store franchisee, David Wangness of Emeryville, California. In October of 1991, the Oakland fire devastated his home and most of his belongings. David, a new franchisee who only had been in business for three months, was attending a regional franchise meeting at the time. His wife, on the other hand, was in the house and managed to escape with only the clothes on her back and their dog.

Immediately upon hearing of the fire and destruction of David's home, fellow franchisees offered to help staff his store. In addition, fellow Northern California Handle With Care Packaging Store franchisees and their franchisor took up a collection to help David furnish an apartment and supply his family with the necessities to get back on their feet. (When I asked David if he had any advice for fellow franchisees in light of such a disaster, he strongly suggested that they make sure to have a back-up set of records in a very safe place.)

The moral of the story tells us to use the advice and wisdom of fellow franchisees nationwide to make the franchised business better, stronger, and more prosperous. It is essential to bear in mind that franchising not only consists of a parent company along with franchisees, it is people like ourselves who took a risk to improve our lives and the lives of our families. This common denominator turns a franchise into a family. The qualities of mutual support and comraderie are the cornerstone to a successful franchise. The case of David Wangness illustrates the importance of cooperation. Success in franchising surpasses the individual unit. As the case of David Wangness shows, ultimate success reflects a solid team effort.

ENDNOTES

[1] Champ Clark, *Flood*, Time-Life Books, Alexandria, VA, 1982.

[2] Ibid.

[3] "How to Make Your House an Ideal Energy Home," Public Service Company, Denver, Colorado, 1991.

[4] "He's Hero of Storm Victims," *Denver Post*, September 13, 1992.

[5] "Destructive Andrew Raises Lumber Prices to Record High," *Rocky Mountain News*, Sept. 3, 1992.

[6] "Getting To Work After The Quake," *Fortune*, Nov. 20, 1992.

[7] "Volcano, The Eruption of Mount St. Helens," written and edited by the combined staffs of the *Daily News*, Longview, Washington, and *The Journal America*, Bellevue, Washington, 1980.

[8] Jon Erickson, *Volcanos and Earthquakes*, Tab Books, Inc., 1988, pp. 276-279.

Conclusion

There has never been a better opportunity to enter the business world under the auspices of franchising. The array of businesses available as franchises boggles the mind. From the traditional fast-food, automotive, and retail franchises, there are opportunities today in the business consulting field, marketing, medical and health-related, as well as the recreational and interior design arenas. You can buy relatively low-cost service franchises or invest in territorially based, capital-intensive, sophisticated businesses. You can enter into a single-unit operation and expand to multiple units over years. You can run a small operation and oversee day-to-day events. You also can opt to employ a chief operating officer, an accounting team, or other trained professionals and run a major business enterprise.

An Arthur Andersen study indicates that sales in business format franchises are expected to increase 14.7 percent during 1992, compared with an estimated growth in the U.S. economy of slightly over 1 percent.

What is important is that along with this predicted growth is significant success and stability. The same study reports that 96.9 percent of all franchises opened within the last five years are still operated by the original franchise owner. Leonard Schwartz, former managing director of Arthur Andersen's franchise consulting services division, now president and CEO of High Tech Signs in Dallas,

Texas, says "Corporate workforce reductions, shifts in human and financial resources, changing consumer needs and the rising appeal of entrepreneurship are fueling franchising growth in the U.S."

Gregg M. Reynolds, Chairman of the International Franchise Association's Educational Foundation, has said that, "This record of achievement among franchise businesses, in the face of the recession, is a strong testament to the hard work, entrepreneurial drive, and creativity of thousands of franchisors and franchisees."

At whatever level you commit to your franchised business, remember you're a member of a team pulling in the same direction. Your franchisor has made a commitment on your behalf. You too have made a commitment to perform on behalf of all the participants in your franchise. Your excellence will rub off on your fellow franchisees.

The franchisor cannot do it all for you. There are no absolute guarantees of success. Allowing that your franchisor performs at a 100 pecent level of commitment, there are still elements of the business that rely primarily on your contribution.

It is the goal of this book to give you the tools to succeed. If you pick up the ball and run with it, fully utilizing the "official" operations manual of your franchise and enhancing it with your improved perspective, you can succeed beyond your original dreams. By meeting competition head on, as well as benefiting from better management techniques, you too can have a successful chapter in this American business success story known as franchising.

Appendix

STATE REGULATIONS

The Following is a summary of the states which have legislation which directly concerns general business format franchising (along with Alberta, Canada) as well as pertinent government bodies to contact. States not mentioned have no statute of general applicability. (Auto, truck, beer, liquor and gasoline marketing legislation has been omitted.) For further details of state laws and other franchise legislation see "Franchising" by Glickman. Matthew Bender & Company. (235 E. 45th St., New York, NY, 10017.)

ARKANSAS: Franchise Practices Act prevents termination of franchisee without good cause and governs renewal of franchise contract. Forbids fraud and deceit in sale of franchises.

CALIFORNIA: Franchise Investment Law requires registration and disclosure by franchisor. The modification of Existing Franchise amendment makes a material modification of an existing franchise the equivalent of a sale subject to the disclosure and registration provisions of the Franchise Investment Law. Another amendment, the Franchisee's Right to Join Trade Association, makes it a violation of the Act for a franchisor to restrict the right of franchisees to join a trade association or to prohibit free association among franchisees for any lawful purposes. The Seller Assisted Marketing Plan statute requires certain sellers of business opportunities to register with the Secretary of State (Legal Review) a disclosure statement and its salesmen before advertising or selling an opportunity and to give each purchase, at lease forty-eight hours prior to the execution of any agreement or the receipt of consideration, a copy of the disclosure statement (franchises covered by the Franchise Investment Law are excluded). Franchise Relations Act covers termination and renewal of franchisee. It prevents termination without good cause and requires franchisor to give 180 days notification to franchisee if the franchisor does not intend to renew contracts and prohibits converting a non-renewed franchise to a company owned unit without compensating the franchisee. (Good Cause is defined as including but not limited to the failure of the franchisee to comply with any lawful requirements of the franchise agreement after being given notice and a reasonable opportunity, which in no event need be more than 30 days, to cure the failure). Contact: Department of Corporations, 3700 Wilshire Blvd., Ste. 600, Los Angeles, CA, 90010. Tel: (213) 736-2741.

CONNECTICUT: Registration and disclosure by franchisor under Business Opportunity Investment Act. Franchising Fairness Law governs termination and non-renewal. Contact: Department of Banking, Securities Division, 44 Capitol Ave., Hartford, CT, 06106. Tel: (203) 566-4560.

DELAWARE: Under Prohibited Trade Practices the Franchise Security Act prohibits unjust or bad faith termination of franchisee or refusal to renew a franchise.

FLORIDA: Franchises and Distributorship Law forbids intentional misrepresentation in the sale of franchises and distributorships. Contact: Consumer Services Div., 209 Mayo Bldg., Tallahassee, FL, 32399-0800. Tel: (904) 488-2221. Business Opportunity Act requires registration and disclosure by franchisor. Contact: Department of Legal Affairs, Consumer Division, 508 Mayo Bldg., Tallahassee, FL, 32399. Tel: (904) 488-2221.

GEORGIA: Business Opportunity statute aimed at preventing fraudulent and deceptive practices in the sale of business opportunities. Governs disclosure and registration. Office of Consumer Affairs, 2 Martin Luther King Dr., Ste. 356, Plaza Level East, Atlanta, GA, 30334. Tel: (404) 656-4731. The Georgia Sale of Business Opportunities Act may include certain franchisors and sub-franchisors depending on whether the exemption under the law applies.

HAWAII: Franchise Investment Law outlines registration, disclosure, termination and renewal. Contact: Department of Commerce and Consumer Affairs, P.O. Box 40, Honolulu, HI, 96810. Tel: (808) 586-2722.

ILLINOIS: A Franchise Disclosure Act regulates disclosure, registration, termination and non-renewal. Contact: Franchise Division, Attorney General's Office, 500 S. Second St., Springfield, IL, 62706. Tel: (217) 782-4465.

INDIANA: Registration Disclosure statute. Deceptive Franchise Practices Act regulates the terms of franchise agreements and practices arising out of the relationship under the contracts. Contact: Securities Commissioner, 302 W. Washington St., Ste. E111, Indianapolis, IN, 46204. Tel: (317) 232-6681.

IOWA: Business Opportunity Act governing disclosure and registration.

KENTUCKY: Business Opportunity Disclosure and Registration Act.

LOUISIANA: Business Opportunity Sellers and Agents Act.

MAINE: Business Opportunity Act outlines registration and disclosure requirements for sale of any business opportunity. Contact: Department of Business Regulations, Special Opportunities Section, State House Station 121, Augusta, ME, 04333. Tel: (207) 582-8760.

MARYLAND: Franchise Registration and Disclosure Law. Contact:

MICHIGAN: Franchise Registration, Disclosure, Pyramid Sales statute includes termination, renewal provision. Contact: Attorney General Department, Consumer Protection Division, 525 W. Ottawa, Lansing, MI, 48913. Tel: (517) 373-7117. Michigan Franchise Investment Law Reform Act.

MINNESOTA: Franchisor Registration, Disclosure, Pyramid, Unfair Practices Act. Contact: Department of Commerce, 133 E. 7th St., St. Paul, MN, 55101. Tel: (612) 296-6328.

MISSOURI: Termination, Renewal, Pyramid Sales statute.

NEBRASKA: Franchise Practices Act governs termination and renewal. Business Practices Act governs seller-assisted marketing plans. Contact: Division of Securities, P.O. Box 95006, Lincoln, NE, 68509-5006. Tel: (402) 471-2171.

NEW HAMPSHIRE: Distributorship Disclosure Act governs registration and disclosure. Contact: Consumer Protection and Antitrust Bureau, 25 Capital St., Concord, NH, 03301. Tel: (603) 271-3641.

NEW JERSEY: Franchise Practices Act concerns termination and renewals.

NEW YORK: Franchise Registration/Disclosure Statute. Contact: New York State, Department of Law, Room 23-122, New York, NY, 10271. Tel: (212) 341-2211. Also Consumer Protection Law Regulation 46 for New York City. Contact: Assistant Commissioner, Legal Affairs, Susan Kassapian, 42 Broadway, New York, NY, 10004. Tel: (212) 487-4418.

NORTH CAROLINA: Business Opportunities Sales Law requires disclosure. Contact: Secretary of State, Securities Division, 300 N. Salsbury St., Room 404, Raleigh, NC, 27611. Tel: (919) 733-3924.

NORTH DAKOTA: Franchise Investment Law governs registration, disclosure, termination and renewal. Contact: Securities Commission, 5th Floor, 600 East Boulevard, Bismarck, ND, 58505. Tel: (701) 224-2910.

OHIO: Business Opportunity Purchasers Protection Act. Contact: Assistant Attorney General, Consumer Frauds & Crime Section, State Office Tower, 25th Floor, 30 E. Broad St., Columbus, OH, 43266-0410. Tel: (614) 466-8831.

OKLAHOMA: Business Opportunity Sales Act.

OREGON: Franchise and Distributorship Investment Regulation Act requires disclosures from franchisor. Contact: Department of Insurance and Finance, Div. of Finance and Corporate Securities, Securities Section, 31 Labour & Industries Building, Salem, OR, 97310. Tel: (503) 378-4387.

RHODE ISLAND: Franchise Disclosure (Anti-Misrepresentation) statute requires full disclosure. Contact: State of Rhode Island, Department of Business Regulation, Securities Division, 233 Richmond St., Ste. 232, Providence Rhode Island, 02903-4232. Tel: (401) 277-3048.

SOUTH CAROLINA: Business Opportunity Sales Act covers disclosure. Contact: Attn: Charles E. Brown, Secretary of State's Office, P.O. Box 11350, Columbia, SC, 29201. Tel: (803) 734-2169.

SOUTH DAKOTA: The South Dakota Franchise Law requires registration and disclosure. Contact: Franchise Administrator, Division of Securities, 910 East Sioux, State Capital Building, Pierre, SD, 57501. Tel: (605) 773-4823.

TEXAS: Business Opportunity Act requires disclosure and registration. (Franchisors who comply with F.T.C. requirements are exempt.)

UTAH: Business Opportunity Act requires a disclosure statement.

VIRGINIA: Retail Franchising Act covers termination, renewal, registration and disclosure. Contact: Examination Coordinator, Franchise Section, Division of Securities and Retail Franchising, P.O. Box 1197, Richmond, VA, 23209. Tel: (804) 786-7751. Also: Business Opportunities Disclosure Act.

WASHINGTON: Franchise Investment Protection Act requires disclosure and registration. It also governs termination and renewal. Contact: Department of Licensing, P.O. Box 9033, Olympia, WA, 98507-9033. Tel: (206) 753-6928. Also: Business Opportunity Fraud Act covering disclosure and registration.

WISCONSIN: Franchise Investment Law requires registration and disclosure. Contact: Securities Commission, P.O. Box 1768, Madison, WI, 53701. Tel: (608) 266-3364. Also Dealership Practices Act covers termination and renewal.

PUERTO RICO: Dealer's Contracts Law covering termination and non-renewal of contract.

ALBERTA, CANADA: The Franchises Act requires registration and disclosure. Contact: Deputy Director for Franchises, Alberta Securities Commission, 21st Floor, 10025 Jasper Ave., Edmonton, AB, T5J 3Z5. Tel: (403) 427-5201.

Franchising and Business Glossary

Accounting Profit – Any amount earned in excess of the cash amount invested to earn it.

Advertising Fee – An annual fee paid by the franchisee to the franchisor for corporate advertising expenditures; usually less than 3 percent of the franchisee's annual sales. Usually paid in addition to the royalty fee. Not all franchisors charge advertising fees.

Area Franchise – (a.k.a. Development Agreement, Master Franchise) A franchise granted to develop a defined geographical area. May include performance schedule and sub-franchising rights.

Anti-Trust –The laws and legal actions designed to insure fair trade and competition and to prevent business monopolies.

Bond – Certificates or evidence of debt issued by corporations and governments involving a promise to pay a certain amount of money on a specific date and interest at a stated rate.

Budget – a plan for the use of money based on goals and expected income and expenditures.

Business Format Franchising – The franchisor licenses the franchisee to use product, service, and trademark, and also teaches the franchisee the entire business format, including marketing, selling, inventory, accounting, personnel procedures, etc. Furthermore, the franchisor provides support via training and communications to the franchisee for the duration of their business relationship. Restaurants, retail, and many service businesses are business format franchisors.

Capital – Wealth in the form of cash and securities or property and equipment that can be used to produce or create more wealth.

Capital Goods – The tools, equipment, and machinery used to produce other goods or to provide services.

Capital Investments – An expenditure for plant or equipment that adds to the value of the property of a business, rather than for operating expenses.

Capital Resources – Capital resources refer to products people make to create other goods. These include mining equipment, drilling rigs, processing plants, and all of the tools, machines, buildings, and equipment used to develop, produce, process, and distribute energy.

Caveat Emptor – Let the buyer beware (Latin).

Caveat Venditor – Let the seller beware (Latin).

Common Stock – a share in the ownership of a corporation.

Company – association of persons who have come together with capital, skills, and time to perform some commercial action such as production, distribution, selling, promoting, franchising, etc.

Company-Owned Outlet – Some franchisors establish company-owned stores or offices that in appearance are identical to the franchised outlets.

Competition – Continuing struggle among business firms to gain a larger share of a given market or for other business advantages.

Consumer – One who uses goods and services; buyer of goods and services.

Conversion Franchising – The conversion of established, existing, independent outlets to franchised outlets.

Copyright – The exclusive right of a person to use, and to license others to use, an intellectual property such as a book, pamphlet, or other published material.

Corporation – A legal entity created under law that may enter into agreements, carry on business activities, perform a variety of functions, and be subject to legislation and law suits.

Customer – One who buys or does business with a particular store or firm. Person who makes a purchase.

Debenture – Usually an unsecured promise to pay, issued by a corporation or company.

Depreciation – A decrease in the value of an item over a period of time due to age, wear, and use.

Disclosure – Revealing facts to others. In the sense used herein, these facts may be complimentary to the franchisor or may be uncomplimentary, such as disclosing a prior bankruptcy.

Disclosure Document – All franchisor companies are required by the Federal Trade Commission (FTC) to provide this document to prospective franchisees at the first personal meeting to discuss the sale of the franchise, and at least 10 business days prior to the prospective franchisee signing a franchise agreement, or paying the franchisor money to buy the franchise. The document aids the prospective franchisee's evaluation of the franchisor company. The content is regulated by the FTC and/or state regulatory authorities.

Distributorship – A right granted by a manufacturer or wholesaler to sell a product to others. A distributorship is normally not a franchise.

Dividend – The amount of money paid out of earnings or proceeds from the sale of property that is divided among shareholders or creditors. It usually represents a share of profits paid in proportion to the share of ownership.

Economics – The study that deals with the production, distribution, and consumption of goods and services and the related subjects of labor, finance, and taxation.

Entrepreneur – A person who assumes the risk and responsibility for starting and operating a business.

Equity Shares – Securities (stocks) representing an ownership interest in the issuing company.

Exclusive Territory – The geographical area owned by a franchisee. When definite boundaries for trading or selling are specified in the franchise agreement, the franchisee must refer customers from outside his or her boundary to a fellow franchisee who owns those territorial rights.

Feasibility Analysis – A study that considers factors in the marketplace and draws conclusions as to whether a program or product can be profitably and economically pursued.

Federal Trade Commission (FTC) – The U.S. government agency that regulates franchising. The main office is located in Washington, D.C.; there are regional offices throughout the country.

Financial Institution – A business engaged in money saving, lending, and borrowing for the purpose of channeling funds into investments for productive activities.

Fiscal Policy – Federal government action or taxation, spending, and public debt designed to promote full employment, price stability, and economic growth.

Franchise – An agreement, whether written or oral, for consideration by which a person permits the distribution of goods or services under this trademark, service mark, or tradename, during which time the grantor retains control over others or renders significant assistance to others. (This definition is substantially that of the Federal Trade Commission. See the Final Interpretive Guides, Federal Register, Vol. 44, No 166, Friday, August 14, 1979, p. 49.996 et seq.) Counsel also should research definitions in controlled jurisdictions, applicable case law, and formal and informal opinions rendered by state and federal regulatory authorities.

Franchise Advisory Council – A group formed by the franchisor to provide feedback from the franchisee's perspective.

Franchise Agreement – Sets forth the expectations and requirements of the franchisor. Describes the franchisor's commitment to the franchisee. Includes information about territorial rights of the franchisee, location requirements, training schedule, fees, general obligations of the franchisee, general obligations of the franchisor, etc.

Franchise Association – A group formed by the franchisees to deal collectively with the franchisor.

Franchises by Type –

> A. *Trade Name Franchise*: This type of franchise concept involves primarily the use of a registered trade name, service mark, or patented product protected by registration.

> B. *Business Format (Operating Systems Franchise)*: This franchise concept is based on a protected housemark and a specific operating system that must be followed by the franchise owner.

> C. *Conversion Franchise*: This is a franchise that permits existing businesses to join a national franchise system to use its recognized name and trademark.

Franchise Fee – A one-time fee paid by the franchisee to the franchisor to "buy into" the franchise. Generally the fee reimburses the franchisor for the costs of initial training and support for new franchisees.

Franchisee – A person to whom the right to conduct a business is granted by the franchisor (see definition of Person below).

Franchising – Neither an industry nor a business, but a method of doing business within a given industry. At least two parties are involved in franchising; the franchisor and the franchisee. Technically, the contract binding the two parties is the franchise.

Franchisor – A person issuing or granting a franchise (see definition of Person below).

Housemark – A trademark used to identify the commercial operations of a company, and may also be the company name (Dupont). The name may be used to identify one or more product(s) and may be used in combination with other trademarks or tradenames.

Identity Items – Those items (such as paper products, uniforms, ashtrays, or exterior signs) usually required to be used in a franchisee's business, which display the trademarks of the franchisor.

Income Tax – a tax on the net income of individuals and businesses.

Insurance – a way of spreading and sharing financial risks: a form of contract called a policy, in which the insurer agrees to pay an agreed amount of money to the insured in the event of certain financial losses resulting from specific hazards or perils outlined in the policy.

Initial Investment/Unencumbered Capital – Usually includes the franchise fee and the amount of capital required to commence operating a franchise.

International Franchise Association (IFA) – Trade association for franchisors. Based in Washington, D.C., the IFA requires its members to follow a rigid code of ethics.

Inventory – Goods, possessions, and property on hand.

Investment – The act of putting money into property or securities for the purpose of receiving income or for appreciation in value.

Management – The process of organizing and utilizing resources to accomplish predetermined objectives; also the administrative aspect of an industry as opposed to labor.

Marketing – The many different activities that are involved in moving goods from producers to consumers. In its broadest sense, this includes selling, advertising, packaging, public relations, market research, merchandising, and other related activities.

Marketing Plan (Franchise) – A technique by which franchises are to be sold. Includes the number of sales anticipated within a series of time periods (first year, second year, etc.), to whom those sales are to be made (profile of the individual, area franchising, sub-franchising), and the anticipated geographical expansion of the franchise system.

Markets (Supply & Demand) – The market responds to all of the individual decisions made by people, businesses, and various government agencies.

Master Franchisee – Describes an individual or company that owns the exclusive rights to develop a particular territory for the franchisor company by selling franchises to third parties.

Money – A medium of exchange that is widely circulated and generally accepted as a standard of value for a society.

National Alliance of Franchisees (NAP) – A national coalition organized in 1977 to represent and protect the interest and rights of franchisees. National headquarters are in Washington, D.C.

Offer – An oral or written proposal to sell a franchise to a prospective franchisee upon understood general terms and conditions. Note: Under state and federal regulations, the term "offer" is broader than the common law contract law definition.

Operating Cost – Expenses connected with the normal operations of a business, excluding non-operating expenses such as debt, reserves for taxes, etc.

Operating Manual – For comprehensive guidelines advising a franchisee how to operate the franchised business. It covers all aspects of the business, including general business procedures not necessarily peculiar to the franchised business. It may be separated into different manuals addressing such subjects as accounting, personnel, advertising, promotion, and maintenance.

Person – An individual, partnership, or corporation.

Product – The result or end of some process of production or manufactured or processed items as opposed to services, or to goods or commodities in their natural state.

Product Franchising – Selling the right to distribute a particular product. This is the way franchising began with Singer, General Motors, and Coca Cola.

Productivity – The amount of production as related to the effort required to produce it.

Profit – In a free-market economy, the opportunity to earn a profit is the main reason for starting a business or increasing production. Profit is what remains after all the costs of production, distribution, and taxes have been deducted from the price consumers are willing to pay.

Pro Forma – A balance sheet or profit and loss statement that assumes levels of revenue and expense, capital assets, liabilities, and net worth. Pro forma statements issued by the franchisor to the franchisee should be based on existing historical operating results.

Prototype Business – A business site developed and used by the franchisor to develop and test new ideas. In service businesses, the prototype is the original or perfected operation.

Pyramid – A so-called business where the focus is on selling the right to sell a product versus selling the product itself.

Qualification Checklist – A document prepared by the franchisor to be completed by the prospective franchisee that provides the initial information to the franchisor in order to assist him in determining whether the prospect is capable and motivated. A financial statement is almost always included in the checklist format.

Quality Control – The method by which the franchisor enforces the rules of operation set forth in the operating manual. Quality control implies traveling inspectors who visit each franchisee and check the operation of the franchised operation.

Registration – A requirement in several states that requires specific information be submitted and approved by state regulatory authorities before franchises may be offered in that state. As compared to "disclosure" (see above), material contained in the registration is more extensive. For example, a bond, fingerprints, and pictures of principal officers may be required in certain jurisdictions. Note: The Federal Trade Commission has no provision for registration, thus the franchisor need only prepare an accurate and complete disclosure document conforming to the FTC regulations.

Research & Development (R&D) – A systematic investigation to establish basic facts, to discover new principles, and to develop new methods and/or products. This role is traditionally assumed by the franchisor in franchising.

Risk – An element of uncertainty or possibility of loss.

Rules of Operation – Specific mandatory rules with which every franchisee and company outlet must comply. This document will change from time to time. By specific reference in the franchise agreement, violation of the Rules of Operation permits the franchisor to cancel a franchise agreement.

Service Mark – The specific statutory definition (15 U.S.C. Sec. 1127) states ". . . a mark used in the sale of advertising of services of one person and distinguish them from the services of others." The word "trademark" is specifically associated with goods or products such as toothpaste or automobiles, whereas service marks relate to employment agencies, real estate chains, and the like. They are both of equal stature and are afforded the same protection under the law.

Sherman Anti-Trust Act – 15 U.S.C., Sec. 1-7, as amended (1976); provides, in general, that it is illegal to conspire, by contract or otherwise, to restrain trade. Franchisee associations must be carefully monitored and franchise agreements drafted, except under certain case law exceptions, to avoid allocation of territories or fixing prices. As it affects franchising, the Sherman Act is applied to activities within a single state, whereas the Robinson-Patman Act can only apply to matters involved in two or more states (interstate commerce). The basic antitrust statutes have evolved since 1890 and each body of law has been enlarged and modified by the subsequent acts, some of which you will find in this glossary. There are other anti-trust acts, notably the Federal Trade Commission Act, The Clayton Act, and the state anti-trust laws and "Little" FTC acts. In order to avoid anti-trust problems, seek adequate legal counsel.

Slick – A pre-prepared piece of advertising material usually composed by the franchisor for the franchisee for use in local print media. It is "camera ready" meaning that newspapers or other media can use it without significant additional cost to franchisees for composition and makeup.

Sub-Franchise Agreement – A franchise granted to develop or sell a person's franchise rights to a third party in a defined geographical area. A portion of the franchise fee is normally paid in advance for a certain minimum number of franchise outlets that may be activated by the developer or sold at a profit by the developer (sub-franchisors) to an individual franchise buyer. The sub-franchisor (developer) normally receives a share of the initial full franchise fee and a percentage of the royalty payment, advertising fees, or special training fees that are paid to the franchisor. In return, certain responsibilities, mutually agreed upon, are deeded to the sub-franchisor.

Standardization – The setting of basic standards or specifications that products and/or services must meet. An essential part of franchising.

Supply – The amount of goods and services that will be for sale at various prices at stated times.

Total Investment – The amount of money estimated for complete set-up of a franchisee's business, including the initial investment, working capital, and subsequent additions to inventory and equipment deemed necessary for a fully operational and profitable enterprise.

Trademark – The name associated with a product (see Service Mark). Prior to federal registration, the symbol "TM" or "SM" may be affixed near the word or words constituting the mark or symbol, to inform the public that it is intended that the name be protected.

Trade Secret (a.k.a. proprietary product or service) – Knowledge in the possession of the franchisor that is revealed to the franchisee by the franchise transaction. Trade secrets may take the form of construction or operating procedures, a formula for the mix or ingredient to prepare food, or the classical customer list. Appropriate legal provisions written into the franchise agreement, such as a covenant not to compete, are important in protecting these secrets.

Turnkey – The franchisor is responsible for fully developing a "turnkey" franchise until, or after, the doors are open for business.

Tying – Forcing a franchisee to purchase one product as a condition to the sale of another. Tying may be illegal if the products used in the franchise operation can be acquired from other sources at a more competitive price. The product must, however, be judged "equal to or better than" the product specified by the franchisor in terms of quality.

Uniform Franchise Offering Circular (U.F.O.C.) – A form of disclosure document containing required information supplied by the franchisor to the franchisee. Initially promulgated by the Midwestern Securities Commissioners to provide a uniform method of disclosure for the benefit of franchisor and franchisee, its use is permitted in non-regulated states by FTC Rule 436.

Vertical and Horizontal Competition – Applicable principally to price-fixing or tying arrangements. Vertical connection deals with a buyer-seller relationship, as in franchisor-franchisee (see Tying). Horizontal restraints of trade in franchising arrangements are among a group of franchisees (sometimes including company-owned outlets) in a defined and homogeneous geographical area. Also, in franchising, horizontal competitors are those offering a franchise or franchise product similar in price, whereas vertical competitors are similar in product or service, but not in price.

Recommended Reading to Check Out a Franchise

Consult these sources of information on individual franchise companies and the franchising industry in general:

Franchise Opportunities Handbook. Superintendent of Documents, U.S. Dept. of Commerce, Washington, DC 20402.

Franchising in the Economy. 1983–1985, U.S. Dept. of Commerce (address above).

International Franchise Association Directory of Membership. 1984–1985. IFA, 1025 Connecticut Ave., N.W., Suite 797, Washington, DC 20036. If you ask, the IFA will refer you to advisers or consultants in various areas of franchising.

Is Franchising for You? Learn Before You Buy. Set of six audio tapes. Franchise Learning and Consulting Center, 10 Lottingtown Road, Glen Cove, NY 11542.

Robert E. Bond, *The Source Book of Franchise Opportunities*, Dow Jones-Irwin, 1818 Ridge Road, Homewood, IL 60430.

Financial Reference Books

The Power of Money Dynamics. Author: Venita Van Caspel.

Megatrends. Author: John Naisbitt.

Sources of Additional Informaiton on Franchising

Small Business Administration
Office of Business Development
1441 L Street, N.W.
Washington, DC 20014

Council of Better Business Bureaus, Inc.
1150 17th Street, N.W.
Washington, DC 20036

Dun and Bradstreet
(for credit analysis)

Federal Trade Commission
Bureau of Enforcements
6th St. & Pennsylvania Ave., N.W.
Washington, DC 20580

International Franchise Association
1350 New York Ave., Suite 900
Washington, DC 20005

The Information Franchise Newsletter
Info. Press
736 Center Street
Lewiston, NY 14092

Franchise Opportunity Handbook
Franchising in the Economy
(available from the International Franchise Association)

Index

A

Account(s)
  see Checking, Credit card, Savings
  payable, 89, 130-131
  receivable, 39, 89, 124, 129, 130,
    133-134
Accountant, 9, 110, 113, 123, 143
Accounting, 4
Accumulating cash value, 50
Ace Hardware, 189
Acquisition, 140
  see Merger and acquisition
Added value, 31
ADI, *see* Area of dominant influence
Advertisements, 98
Advertising, 30, 34, 65, 97, 99-100,
    112, 123
  see Pooled, Subliminal
  campaign, 115
  expert advice, 100-101
  funds, management, 142-143
  programs, 142
Advertising to Women (ATW), 100
Advisory
  councils, *see* Franchise
  team, 64
Age composition, changes, 82
AMBIC, 12-13
American
  Banker's Insurance, 96
  Family Doctor, 126
  Hospital Association, 38

  Speedy Printing Centers, 57
Americans with Disabilities Act, 127
Anderson, Arthur, 203
Arby's, 46, 70
Area
  developer, 29
  development, 55
Area of dominant influence (ADI),
    102
Armed robbery, 169-170
Assets, 40, 43, 89, 129
Assistance, 32
  see Local
Athlete's Foot, 189
ATW, *see* Advertising to Women
Auto industry, franchis pioneer, 5-6
Automation, 125
Avco Financial Services, 143

B

Bad checks, 172-173
Bad debt
  allowance, 136
  insurance, 134
Balance sheet, 40, 42, 89
  preparation/analysis, 143
Bank
  see Commercial, Money
  credit, 43
  income, 38
  loans, 38-40

payroll services, 143
Bank of America, 143
Banker, 40
    see Personal
Bankruptcy, 8, 9, 24
Bargains, 125
Barter, *see* Corporate
Bartering, 156
Bid(s), accepting process, 153-154
Bidding, 161
Bill(s), *see* Short-term, U.S.
Billing, 134
    see Discount, Unpaid
Blind pool, 56
Blockbuster, 68, 91
Body Shop, The, 70
Bond, *see* Industrial, Tax-free, U.S.
Boom cycle, 87
Borrowing
    see Money
    creativity, 58
Brand name recognition, 19
Break-in, 165, 166
Bridge financing, 51
Broker, *see* Franchise
Budget, *see* Business, Marketing
Budgeting, *see* Cash
Bureau of the Census, 99
Bureau of National Affairs, 180
Burger King, 33, 69, 84, 85, 113, 196
Burglar alarms, 165, 166
Burglarproofing, 165-166
Burglary, 163-165
Business(es)
    see Established, Mobile-based,
        Niche, Service
    budget, 41
    conditions, 17
    consultant, 11
    consulting services, 106
    cost, 121
    see Crime
    cycles, monitoring, 85-87
    experience, 9
    format, 4

franchise/franchising, 24-26
interruption, 154
insurance, 198
manager, 144
margins, 39
philosophy, 22
plan, 41, 43, 47, 52
    see Start-up
ravages, 185-201
safe, 168-169
self-investment, 140-141
system, 19
volume, 122
Business-to-business sales, 21
Bust cycle, 87

C

Capital, 11, 16
    see Financing, Private, Venture,
        Working
    conservation, 54
    equipment, 112
    growth, 51
    infusion, 38
    sources, 37, 41, 50
Capitalization, 43
    see Recapitalization
Carl, Kim, 177
Cash, 145-146
    budgeting, 41, 136-139
    disbursements, 89
    management, 139
    receipts, 89
    retention, 129
    value, *see* Accumulating
Cash flow, 53, 58, 129, 133, 134,
        136-139
    analysis, 88
    charting, 42
    problems, 137
    projections, 40, 47
    records, 88
    statements, 89

Casualty insurance agents, 110
Catalfamo, Lee, 12-13
CD, *see* Certificate, Negotiable
CDC, *see* Certified, 504
Census, *see* Bureau
Century 21, 190
Certificate of deposit (CD), *see* Negotiable
Certified Development Company (CDC), *see* 504
Chambers of Commerce, 99
Charles of the Ritz, 95
Check(s), *see* Bad
Checking account, 38
Chrysler, 96
Claim disallowance, 158
Client base, 30
Collateral, 39, 42, 47
Collection, 133
   agency, 135
   recommendations, 134
Commercial bank, 37, 51, 145
   loan, 38
Commercial insurance coverage, 197
Commercial lending, 38
Commercial paper, 144
Commissions, *see* Sales
Common carriers, 123
Company
   evaluation, 23
   structure, determination, 41
Company-owned outlet, 32
Compensation, 139-140
Competition, 16, 85, 109
   see Global, Labor, Mail-order
   analysis, 63-77
   benefits, 76-77
   range, identification, 67-69
   staying ahead, 65-66
   understanding, 66-67, 97
Competitive
   franchisor, identification, 64
   pricing, 83-85
   strategy, development, 64
Competitors, 64

analysis, 52
application, 71-72
Comptroller of the Currency, 180
Computerization, 12
Computerland, 189
Conditions, *see* Market
Conference calls/conferencing, 125
Consignment, 53
   purchases, 53
Conservation, 191-192
Consumer
   Product Safety Act, 87
   spending, 87
Continental Airlines, 125
Control, *see* Costs, Managerial, Quality
Contract Loan Program, 45-46
Contractual limitations, 55
Cooling-off period, 33
Corporate
   barter, 59, 156
   management, 24
Corporation, 40, 52, 132, 144
   see Nonprofit
Cost(s), 54, 75
   see Business, Crime, Explicit, Fixed, Full, Historical, Inventory, Labor, Managerial, Merchandising, Opportunity, Overhead, Social, Transaction
   control, 121-128
   management, 121
   savings, 85
Cost per prospect (CPP), 101, 102
Cost per thousand (CPM), 101, 102
Cost-cutting procedures, 121
Cost-plus pricing, 111
Counterfeit money, 171-172
Coupons, 125
CPM, *see* Cost per thousand
CPP, *see* Cost per prospect
Craig, Jenny, 67
Creative Asset Management, 110, 144, 161

Creative Croissants, 152
Credit
  see Bank, Letters, Line, Trade
  availability, 79
  capacity conservation, 54
  card accounts, 39
  card theft, 170-171
  ratings, 130
  risk, 39
  union, 50
Creditors, 130
Creditworthiness, evaluation, 39
Crime
  see White collar
  business cost, 163-183
Customer(s), 68, 84, 102, 110, 114
  see Delinquent
  analysis, 52
  attracting, 41
  base, 114, 122
  service profiles, 41
Cycle, *see* Boom, Business, Bust
Cyr, Rod, 69, 110

D

Dairy Queen, 72
Debt, 54, 137
Decision making, 35, 79, 123
Decorating Den, 103
Decorator Den, 189
Delinquent customers, 135-136
Delivery policies/schedules, 154
Demand, 83
  see Elasticity, Supply and demand
Demographic data, 99
Dessert Cart, 117
Development agreement, 28
Developer, *see* Area
Diet Center, The, 67
Direct mail, 114
Disaster
  see Man-made, Natural
  Program, 46

Disclosure
  document, 8-9, 22, 23, 33
  requirements, 7
Discount
  basis, 144
  billing, 131-132
Discounted pricing, 87, 114
Distribution, 75, 87
  rights, 4, 5
  system, 4, 6
Distributor, 53
Dr. Vinyl, 55, 71
Drought, 185, 189-191
  avoidance steps, 191
Dry-Clean USA, 71
Dunhill Office Personnel, 17

E

8(a) Program, 48
Earning(s)
  capability, 9
  projections, 47
Earthquake, 185, 195
  avoidance steps, 195
Easy Spirit, 100
Economic conditions, 17, 24
Economy
  see Market
  changes, 81
Elasticity of demand, 84-85
Embezzlement, 179-180
Employee, 126, 139
  investment, 141-142
  leasing, 127-128
  resumes, 52
  Stock Option Plan (ESOP), 49-50
  theft, 177-178
Employment, 124
  see Franchising
Energy use, 191-192
Entrepreneur(s), 16, 52, 73
Entrepreneurial skills, 12
Entrepreneurship, 86

Equipment, 89
  see Capital
  leasing, 54
  loan, 38
  obsolescence, 54
Equity
  see Shareholder
  Access Credit Account, 43
  buildup, 54
ESOP, *see* Employee
Established businesses
  business plan, 42-43
Ethics, 22
Everyday low pricing, 116-117
Excessive inventory, storage, 157
Executive wages, 121
Exit clause, 52
Expansion plans, 86
Expense, *see* Operating, Travel
Explicit costs, 113
Export Revolving Line of Credit Pro-
  gram, 45
Express Lube, 55

F

4-Sale Hotline, 70
504 Certified Development Com-
  pany (CDC) Program, 45
Face value, 145
Facilities loans, 38
Fake identification, 173-174
Failure rate, 11
Fairchild, Nancy, 94
Fast food
  franchises, 56, 131
  franchising, 6-7
FDIC, 145
Federal agency securities, 146
Federal District Seal, 172
Federal Home Loan Mortgage Corpo-
  ration (FHLMC)
Federal National Mortgage Associa-
  tion (FNMA), 146

Federal regulation, 8-10
Federal Reserve, 130
  Board, 37, 86
  Board of Governors, 85
  Notes, 171
Federal Trade Commission (FTC), 8,
  10, 24
  rule, 23
  Rule 436, 8, 9
FHLMC, *see* Federal Home
Finance paper, 145
Financial
  consultant, 144
  management, 119-201
  officer, 136
  operations, 119-201
  plan, 41
  products, 110
  report, 40
  reporting, 39
  services, 111
  stability, 24
    see Supplier
  statement, 47
    see Personal
Financials, 52
Financing
  see Bridge
  capital sources, 37-60
Finishing, 75
Fixed costs, 121-122
  controlling, 122-125
  reduction, 123-125
Flooding, 186-188
  avoidance steps, 188
FNMA, *see* Federal National
Foliage Design Systems, 34-35, 94,
  110
  Franchise Advisory Council, 35
  Franchisee Advisory Council, 34,
  69
Forced retirement, 13
Ford, Henry, 6
Forecast timetables, 41
Foreign markets, 34

Franchise
  see Business format, Mobile-
    based, Multiple, Product, Re-
    tail, Single-unit, Trade name
  advantages, 31-32
  advisory councils, 34-35
  broker, use, 21
  Broker's Network, 21
  business, getting started, 1-60
  cancellation, 9
  components, 3
  marketing brochure, 38
  offering circular, 38
  opportunities
    components, 25
    evaluation, 23-24
    handbooks, 20
  Opportunities Handbook, 66
  pioneer, *see* Auto
  relationship, 29-30, 35
  renewal, 9
  risks, 32-33
  selection, 20-21
  teams, 24
  termination, 9
Franchisee
  see Franchising, Unit
  advisory council, 153, 160
  franchising perspective, 19-36
  harmony, 64
  input, 20
Franchisee-franchisor relationship, 29
Franchisee-owned units, 14
Franchising
  see Business, Fast food, Franchi-
    see, International, New
  benefits, 30-31
  boom, 14-17
  employment, 14
  evolution, 3-18
  growth, 10-11
  history, 4
  problems, 7
  questions, 22-23
  success rates, 11

suitability, 13-14
United States, 5
Franchisor
  see Competitive, Franchisee-fran-
    chisor, Prospective, Retail-
    based
  procedures, 22
  responsibility, 20
  teaming, 69
  violation, 10
FSLIC, 145
FTC, *see* Federal Trade Commission
Full cost pricing, 111
Fund(s), *see* Initial, Recurring
Funding by leasing, 54

G

General Business Services, 134
General Motors, 5-6, 12
General Nutrition Centers, 189
General partner, 57
Glass Doctor, 55, 71
Global
  competition, 12
  economy, 75
  marketplace, 75-76
Glossary, 205-215
Goals, 40
Good will, 19
Government
  see Local
  regulations, 16
  rules, 16
  spending, 79, 87
Grease Monkey, 17, 71
Growth, 24, 52
  see Capital, Market
  plans, 39
  projections plans, 42
  rate, 14
  sales, 114
Guaranteed loan program, 45
Guidelines, 33
  see Staffing, Training

H

Handicapped Assistance Loans, 46
Handle with Care Packaging Store,
    200
Heinz, H.J., 116
Hertz, 7, 190
High Tech Signs, 203
Historical costs, 113
Holiday Inn, 190
Housing and Urban Development
    (HUD), 99
HUD, *see* Housing
Hurricane(s), 185, 193
Hype, 32-33

I

IBM, 12, 13, 14, 30
Identification, *see* Fake, Photo
IFA, *see* International
Illegal rebates, 181
Income, 86
    see Bank
    source, 24
Incremental analysis pricing, 112
Independents, 63, 64, 72
Industrial
    paper, 144
    revenue bonds, 56
    short-term lending, 38
Inflation, 111, 130
In-house departments, 123, 124
Initial
    funds, 9
    public offerings (IPO), 55-56
Innovation, 75
Installment payment, 132
    plan, 131
Institutional investor, 52
Insulation, 192
Insurance, 121, 124, 157, 161

see Bad, Business interruption,
    Casualty, Commercial, In-
    ventory
companies, 96
coverage, 198, 200
firms, 52
planning, 199-201
policies, 41, 50, 125
    reviewing, 125
segmentation, 96
Interest, 131
    loss, 133
    penalties, 134
    rate(s), 56, 85
Internal Revenue Service, 132
International
    developments, 75
    Franchise Association (IFA), 8, 22,
        29
        Educational Foundation, 204
    franchising, 27, 33-34
    House of Pancakes, 6
Inventory, 39, 53, 87, 89, 150, 151
    see Excessive, LAN
    control, 4, 157, 159
        computer use, 159-160
    cost, recognition, 157-158
    management, 140, 149-161
    protection, special insurance, 158-
        159
    reports, 42
    structure, 4
    turnover rate, evaluation, 158
Investment, 51, 104
    see Long-term, Short-term
    program, 110
    type, 38
Investor
    see Institutional
    share, 52
IPO, *see* Initial
ITEX, 156

J

Jiffy Lube, 71

K

Kentucky Fried Chicken (KFC), 6, 7
Key(s), 167-168
Kickbacks, 181
Kroc, Ray, 6, 31
Kunzman, George, 13, 30

L

Labor, 86, 125, 135
    costs, 83
    market, competition, 90
    needs, reassessment, 124
    supply, 90
LAN inventory software, 160
Lease negotiation, 30
Leasing, 123
    see Employee, Equipment, Fund-
        ing
    disadvantages, 54-55
    firm, 127
Lender, *see* Private
Lending, *see* Commercial, Industrial
Lepeep, 83
Letters of credit, 131-132
Leveraged buyouts, 51
Liabilities, 40, 89, 129
    see Product
Licensing system, 3
Life cycle patterns, 82
Light(s), 164, 168
Limited partner, 57
Line of credit, 39, 44, 130, 131, 138
    see Export, Seasonal, Secured, Un-
        secured
Lions (organization), 94
Liquidity, 145

Litigation history, 8, 9
Loan, 37, 130, 131
    see Bank, Commercial, Contract,
        Equipment, Facilities, Guar-
        anteed, Handicapped, No-in-
        terest, Small, U.S.
    amount, 42
    application, 39
    money, 37
    programs, 49
Local
    assistance, 49
    government, assistance, 56-57
Location(s), 26
    see Multiple
Lock(s), 167
Lockbox, 123
Long-term investment, 145-146
Loss, *see* Profit and loss

M

Macroeconomics, 80-82
Magazines, 101, 102
Mail-order competition, 16
Maintenance, 34, 123
    contracts, 34
Management, 11, 22, 43, 56
    see Advertisement, Corporate, Fi-
        nancial, Inventory, Money,
        Purchasing, Senior
    capabilities, 40
    cost, 86
    positions, 40
Manager, *see* Business, Owner/man-
        ager
Managerial
    assistance, 31
    controls, 25
    costs, 113
Man-made disasters, 181
Manufacturer(s), 41
Manville, 14
March of Dimes, 104

Margin, 122, 137
  see Business, Profit
Mark, 25
Market, 40
  see Foreign, Money, Target
  conditions, 17
    changes, 79-92
  domination, 95-96
  economy, 83
  growth, 86
  oversaturation, 73-74
  research, 98-99
  segment, 101
  segmentation, 95-96
  share, 86
  specialization, 74-75
Marketing, 4, 100
  see Positively
  brochure, *see* Franchise
  budget, 98
  conditions, 100
  data, 99
  goals, 93-107
  plan, 30, 42, 97-98
    development, 41
    development steps, 97-98
  recommendations, 100-101
  segmentation theory, 74, 95
  techniques, 16, 73
  tools, 41
Marketplace, 74, 90, 95
  see Global
Martin, John, 116
Martin Marietta, 14
Mass production, 5
Materials, 125
  substitution, 126
Maybelline, 95
McDonald's, 6, 7, 31, 33, 56, 83, 96-97, 190
Media
  see Print
  selection, 71, 101-104, 142
Merchandise, 53, 130, 154, 155, 157, 159

costs, 131
Merchandising, 4, 97
Merger and acquisition opportunities, 52
Merrill, Lynch, Pierce, Fenner & Smith, 43
MICR, 172
Microeconomics, 80, 82-83
Midas Muffler, 190
Mission statement, 97
Mobile-based
  business, 55
  franchise, 70-71
Mole Hole, The, 132, 161, 190
Money, 41, 55, 124
  see Counterfeit, Loan
  borrowing, relatives, 58
  effective management, 129-147
  management, bank services, 143
  market(s), 50
    funds, *see* Tax-free
  Store, 43
  supply, 79
Monopolies, 82
Motivation, 24
  examination, 21-22
Multimixer, 6
Multiple
  franchise
    structure, 26-29
    units, 33
  locations, 19

N

National Association of Negro Professional and Business Women's Club (NAPBWC), 57
National Demographics, 14
National Video, 91
Natural disasters, 185
Negotiable certificates of deposit (CD), 145
Negotiation, 161

see Lease
New franchises, 12-13
New Jersey Economic Development
    Authority (NJEDA), 49
Niche business, 117
NJEDA, *see* New Jersey
No-interest loan, 53
Nonprofit corporation, 93
Norman, Merle, 70
Note, *see* U.S.
Nutri-System, 67, 103

O

Obsolescence, 157
Occupational Safety and Health Act,
    87
Offering circular, *see* Franchise
Office of Women's Business Owner-
    ship, 48
Operating expense, 54
Operations, *see* Financial
Opportunity costs, 112, 113
OSHA, 16
Outlets, 14
    see Company-owned
Over-dependence, 33
Overhead, 111
    costs, 126
Owner/manager, 113
Ownership, 51

P

Pacific Funding Group, 43
Packaging, 97
Packaging Store, The, 13, 30
Pak Mail, 97, 158, 177
Paper, *see* Commercial, Finance, In-
    dustrial
Partner, 47
    see General, Limited, Silent

Partnerships, 52, 57
    see Unique
PASS, *see* Procurement
Patent pool, 5
Payback, 192
    provision, 53
Payment, 132
    plan, *see* Installment
    schedule, 54
Payroll, 138, 143
    see Bank
    date, 89
Pension funds, 145
Pepsico, 116
Personal
    banker, 38
    financial statement, 42
    loan, 39, 89
    property, 39
Personnel, 123
    procedures, 4
Photo identification (ID), 172, 173
Physicians Weight Loss Centers, 67
PIP, *see* Postal
Pizza Hut, 34, 157, 190
Pool
    see Blind
    site selection, 30
Pooled advertising power, 19
POM, *see* Positively
Position, determination, 98
Positively Outrageous Marketing
    (POM), 105-106
Postal Instant Press (PIP), 34, 189,
    192, 193, 194
Pratt's Guide to Venture Capital
    Sources, 53
Premium pricing, 113-116
Present value, 54
Pressed 4 Time, 55, 71
Price(s), 154-155
    differential, 101
    guarantees, 150
    negotiation, 153
    wars, 84, 117

Pricing
see Competitive, Cost-plus, Discounted, Everyday, Full, Incremental, Premium, Value
components, 110-111
strategies, 109
Principal(s), 40
Print media, 101
Private
capital, 43-44
lender, 45
Procurement Automated Source System (PASS), 48
Producers, 97
Product, 25, 34, 71, 98
see Uniform
development, 70
duplication, 72
franchises, 26
liability, 80
loyalty, 116
production cost, 112-113
sales, 24
substitution, 126
variety, 154
Production, 75, 86, 121, 122, 150
see Product
Profit, 39, 43, 52, 112, 126
margin, 31, 73
projections, 38, 39
sharing funds, 145
Profit and loss statement, 42, 47, 89
Profitability, 30, 39, 93-95, 114, 122
Promotions, 34, 97, 104-105
see Value-added
Prospective franchisor, contact, 22
Proximity alarms, 166
Public
offering, 52
relations, 97, 104-105, 123
Service Electric & Gas, 12
shell, 56
warehouses, 123
Purchase(s), 89
obligation, 9

orders, 160
Purchasing, 131
agent, 155, 156
influencing factors, 150-151
management, 140, 149-161
process, 150
requirements, needs determination, 151-152
staff, 155-156

Q

Quality, 40
assurance, 31
control, 6, 25
Quotations, 155

R

Rack displays, 26
Radio, 102
Shack, 190
Ramada Inn, 190
Realistic expectations, 33
Recapitalization, 51
see Capitalization
Recession, 12, 13, 43, 85, 130
Recognition, see Brand name, Service
Record keeping, 87-89, 121, 127
system requirements, 89
Recurring funds, 9
Registration requirements, 7
Regulation(s), 3
see Federal, Government, State
lack, 7
Re/Max, 190
Rent, 83, 121, 124, 134
Repurchase, 52
Research and development, 32
Resources, 86, 191-192
Restocking, 160-161
Retail

franchises, 132
  outlets, 5
Retail-based franchisor, 30
Retailers, 41
Retirement
  see Forced
  benefits, 50
Revenue(s), 9
  bonds, *see* Industrial
R-factors, 192
Rights, *see* Distribution, Worldwide
Riots, 181
Risk, 12, 24, 126
  see Credit, Franchise
Risk/reward, 24
Risk-taking, 86
Robbery, 163, 165, 166
  see Armed
Rotary Club, 94
Royalties, 24
Rule(s), *see* Government
Rule 436, *see* Federal Trade Commis-
  sion

S

Safeway, 195
Salary, 113, 122
Sale(s), 89
  see Growth
  commissions, 125
  compensation, 123
  potential, determination, 41
  projections, 42
  restriction, 9
  techniques, development, 41
  volume, 111
Sanders, Harlan, 6
Savings, 145
  account, 38
Savings and loan (banks), 130
SBA, *see* U.S.
SBIC, *see* Small Business
SCORE, *see* Service

Sears, 12
Seasonal Line of Credit, 46
Secured line of credit, 39
Securities, *see* Federal agency
Segments, 96
  determination, 98
Selling, 4, 97
Senior management, 64
Service, 98
  see Telephone
  businesses, 41
  Core of Retired Executives
    (SCORE), 99
  marketing plans, 25
  Master, 190
  niche, 85
  production cost, 1112-113
  profiles, *see* Customer
  recognition, 19
Severance packages, 13
Sewing machine war, 5
Shareholder, equity, 89
Shelf life, 159
Sherman, Miguel, 114, 115
Shipping, 75, 150, 158
Shoplifting, 174-176
  avoidance steps, 176
Shortage, 75
Short-term
  investment, 144-145
  Treasury bills, 145
Signs by Tomorrow, 17
Silent partner, 57
Silk Plants, Etc., 73
Silience, 100
Singer Sewing Machine Company, 5
Single-unit franchise, 55
Site selection, 9, 41, 71
  see Pool
Slowdown, 87
Small Business
  Administration, *see* U.S.
  Assistance Centers, 106
  Investment Act of 1958, 51

Investment Companies (SBIC)s, 51, 52
Small claims court, 136
Small loan program, 45
Snowstorms, 196-197
Social
    costs, 113
    values, changes, 82
Software, 88
    see LAN
Specialization, 96-97
Staff
    see Purchasing
    reduction, 122
    survey, 139
Staffing guidelines, 23
Start Now, 110
Start-up business plan, 40-42
State
    Farm insurance, 199
    regulation, 8-10
Stock, 52
Stockholder, 47
Storage, 161
Store layout, 4
Subliminal advertising, 16
Subsidiaries, 51
Success Motivation Institute, 159
SuperCuts, 34, 84, 98, 114, 115
Supplies, 79
Suppliers, 53, 116, 126, 130, 132
    analysis, 52
    contact, 152-153
    dependability, 154
    financial stability, 154
    selection, 152-153
Supply and demand, 82

T

Taco Bell, 116
Target market, 71, 97
    reaching, 61-118
Tasty Taxi, 69

Tax(es), 121, 123
    attorneys, 143
    benefits, 144
    brackets, 144
    credits, 16
    deposits, 138
    preparers, 110
    rates, 79
    reimbursement, 50
    reports, 42
    saving, 55
Taxation, 87
Tax-free
    bonds, 56
    money market funds, 145
Technical assistance, 31
Technological change, 70
Telemarketing, 102
Telephone
    calls, control, 126
    service, 122
Television, 103
Termination, 54
Theft
    see Credit card, Employee
    prevention, 157
Thrift institution, 145
Time
    lapse, 137
    savings, 85
Tornadoes, 185-186
Tort reform, 80
Total Business Systems, 134
Tracking, 140
Trade
    credit, 53
    name franchises, 26
Trademark, 25
Training, 19, 27, 31, 166-168
    guidelines, 23
    period, 31
    program, 9, 25
    time, 144
Transaction cost, 55
Travel expenses, control, 125

About the Author

Carol B. Green is currently the President of Franchise Systems International, Inc., a business consulting firm specializing in franchising. The firm is headquartered in Denver, Colorado. Ms. Green has been involved in franchising since 1968, and has been both a franchisee and a franchisor. She is a widely recognized authority on franchising, and has been quoted in *The Wall Street Journal, Business Age, Dun & Bradstreet Reports, Franchise Update* and numerous other publications.

Ms. Green has been a member of the Board of Directors of the following organizations: SuperCuts, Inc., Three Dee Associates, Inc., Weight Watchers of the Rocky Mountain Region, Inc., The Colorado Association of Commerce and Industry, The Educational Foundation of the Colorado Association of Commerce and Industry, The Greater Denver Chamber of Commerce, The South Suburban Chamber of Commerce, The Governor's Small Business Council, the Lupus Foundation of Colorado and the Health One Foundation. She served as a delegate to the White House Conference on Small Business in 1986. At the White House Conference, she participated on the committee for insurance and tort reform. The delegates considered this to be the number one issue pressing small business.

She is a member of the Committee of 200 and the International Women's Forum. In 1981, Ms Green was recognized by the national Small Business Administration with the Woman-In-Business Advocate award for her numerous business accomplishments.

Shae holds a B.A. in Economics from Loretto Heights College, and previously served on the Board of Trustees of the College